D1682807

RSM McGladrey

McGladrey & Pullen

McGladrey
Beyond the Balance Sheet
1926-2008

by Kathleen Gilbert

Dedication

To our employees—past, present, and future

Foreword

It is a common misconception that the practice of public accounting is all about crunching numbers.

While good public accountants must be able to translate financial information into what it means for a client, they do much more than that. Public accounting is first and foremost about relationships, and today's CPA is often called upon to serve as family counselor, personnel expert, strategic advisor, and communication specialist as well. Accountants are at the heart of business, and no one knows this better than McGladrey.

Founded in Iowa in 1926, McGladrey has grown from modest Midwestern roots into the fifth-largest U.S. provider of accounting, tax, and business consulting services, with more than 7,000 employees in more than 120 offices. Since the turn of the century alone, it has grown from a $300 million firm in 1999 to a $1.4 billion company in 2008. With both a national and international reach, McGladrey touches the lives of people all over the world.

Yet its roots remain vital to its success. As it has grown, McGladrey is proud to have held fast to the culture and values that have sustained it through tremendous changes. This book strives to document that legacy, celebrating the firm's successes and honoring many of the people who helped build the foundation that upholds it today. We hope you enjoy what you find in the following pages and perhaps learn something you may not have known about the company that is McGladrey.

– Kimpa Moss, Mike Kirley, Tom Siders, and Doug Opheim

McGladrey: Beyond the Balance Sheet, 1926-2008

Acknowledgments

If anyone puts to rest the outdated stereotype of the green eyeshade, it is the people of McGladrey. Dynamic, open-minded, and imaginative, they demonstrate that when done right, public accounting is very much a relationship business—a fact that certainly came through in my interaction with members of the firm.

Every person I spoke with was gracious in contributing his or her time and providing thoughtful answers to my questions, and I'd like to acknowledge their invaluable contributions to the work that follows: Dan Brooks, Ivan Bull, Katie Bushard, Larry Dowell, Mitch Gorochow, Tom Horne, Johnnie James, Mike Kirley, LeRoy Martin, Steven Mayer, Diane McNulty, Becky Miller, Kimpa Moss, David Pierce, Doug Opheim, Mark Scally, Dave Scudder, Tom Siders, Connie Smith Benning, Steve Tait, Bill Travis, Jack Wahlig, Dave Wentworth, Bob Wilson, and Jay Zack.

Special thanks go to the members of the book committee—Mike Kirley, Kimpa Moss, Doug Opheim, and Tom Siders—for overseeing the process, providing direction, and reviewing drafts, and to Heather Kriegler for spending countless hours wrangling materials and photos, answering questions, and providing logistical support.

– Kathleen Gilbert

Table of Contents

Chapter One: Made in the Midwest (1926–1977) 1

Chapter Two: Growth Spurts (1977–1999) 21

Chapter Three: A Bold Leap Forward (1999–Present) 47

Chapter Four: Creating Our Future (2008 and Beyond) 69

Appendixes:

    One: How Our EUs Were Built Through Mergers 89

    Two: Historical Timeline 98

    Three: Senior Management and Managing Partners 102

    Four: Board Members 104

    Five: Quotes from RSM CEOs and
          McGladrey & Pullen Managing Partners 106

Our Core Values 108

Published by Heritage Publishers, LLC, Phoenix, AZ
(602) 277-4780 (800) 972-8507 • www.heritagepublishers.com

ISBN 0-929690-94-0
978-0-929960-94-0
Library of Congress Control Number: 2008923318

© 2008 McGladrey

All rights reserved. No part of this publication may be reproduced or transmitted in any form by any means, electronic or mechanical, including photocopying, recording, or by any information storage and retrieval system, without permission.

Printed and bound in the United States of America.

McGladrey: Beyond the Balance Sheet, 1926-2008

Chapter One

Made in the Midwest

(1926-1977)

In the spring of 1919, a tall, thin, dignified-looking 36-year-old World War I veteran arrived for his first day of work in a Des Moines accountant's office dressed in the only set of formal clothes he owned: the United States Army uniform he had recently worn home from France. Ira B. McGladrey had no formal training in accounting; he didn't even have a college degree. But he had worked with numbers as a revenue collector and at a bank and spent about a month as a bookkeeper before the war called him into the army, and he was determined to make accounting his career.

"Up until this time I had turned my hand to a great variety of occupations," he wrote in his autobiography. "I now made up my mind that I would get to be as good as I could at one thing and forget about everything else."

McGladrey had managed to convince the partners at Hawthorne & Widdup, a small local firm, to hire him as a junior accountant despite his lack of experience or training. And in public accounting, the man whose previous occupations included farming, lumbering, school teaching, carpentering, cow-punching, painting, plastering, railroad construction, general merchandising, revenue service, grocery store, banking, and railroad section work, finally found his true calling.

Ira B. McGladrey

A Father's Legacy

Kathleen McGladrey Frey, Ira McGladrey's only child, accepted a Junior Achievement award on behalf of her father in 2005. She traveled 4,000 miles by motor home to get to Iowa to accept the award. An excerpt from her speech follows.

"On behalf of the I. B. McGladrey family, I would like to thank Junior Achievement and the Quad City JA Hall of Fame for this recognition of my father.

"My father followed his 'passions' in life, and if he were here today, he would tell all of you and all of the young people in Junior Achievement programs, that you, too, should follow your passion, which will surely determine a person's success as it did his.

"His other advice to young people today would be to say to them to
- *pursue all educational opportunities to their fullest, and to*
- *work hard and do your best, and to*
- *be honest and truthful, and finally*
- *lead by example in all that you do.*

"In conclusion, I would like to say, to all of the present and former McGladrey partners and employees here tonight, please know that our family is very proud of all that you do. You have been excellent stewards of building upon the legacy that my father started eighty years ago. I. B. McGladrey would be very proud today of all of you and what you have accomplished over these past eighty years."

In less than five years, McGladrey would be a certified public accountant (CPA). Within seven, he would be the proprietor of his own accounting firm. By the end of a distinguished career that spanned more than three decades, he would become a recognized leader in the profession, whose work changed the way accounting was practiced across the nation. He also would leave behind a legacy in the firm bearing his name.

HUMBLE BEGINNINGS

Ira Brown McGladrey was born February 24, 1883, in a small, hand-built cabin near the shores of Lake Superior's Whitefish Bay in Michigan. The McGladrey home was so remote it could be reached only by an arduous hike on a primitive trail through the woods, or via Lake Superior—on a boat in the summer, on the ice in the winter. Despite austere conditions and undeniable poverty, Ira had fond memories of his childhood and later said because their neighbors were just as poor, nobody realized how poor they were.

His parents, Alexander and Mary Jane (Dobbin) McGladrey, were both the children of immigrants and deeply religious Presbyterians who instilled in Ira and his four older brothers the principles of order, honesty, integrity, hard work, and respect for authority that Ira would carry with him for the rest of his life. The family attended church regularly and prayed several times a day. Although Ira's parents had little formal education themselves, they taught their children to read from an early age, using the Bible and other books sent by their parents in Canada. As a result, McGladrey became a voracious reader, especially enjoying books about history and philosophy.

At age 16, Ira passed the state teaching exam and moved to southern Minnesota to teach school and work as a farmhand. Throughout the next two decades, he traveled widely and worked at a variety of jobs across Michigan, Montana, North Dakota, and South Dakota. It was while teaching in Casselton, North Dakota, that he met Bernice McCaul, the blue-eyed daughter of his boardinghouse hosts, whom he married several years later in 1912 while serving as a federal assistant deputy collector of internal revenue for western South Dakota in Aberdeen. Their only child, Kathleen McGladrey, was born on January 28, 1923.

In early March 1917, Ira McGladrey decided to "try my fortune in a bigger city" and moved to Minneapolis, where he secured a job as a bookkeeper for Goodyear Waterproof Co., a manufacturing plant. It proved to be a false start in the accounting field, however. He had been on the job less than a month when Congress declared war on Germany, bringing the United States into the Great War. McGladrey enlisted in the army and rose quickly through the ranks to major. He was on the front when the Germans surrendered. Not surprisingly, when the war finally ended on November 11, 1918, McGladrey—ever the orderly and sober Presbyterian—forwent the celebratory French champagne being guzzled by his fellow soldiers and instead marked the occasion with a quiet game of cards before going to bed.

FINALLY, A CAREER THAT SUITED

After the war, McGladrey approached his new career in public accounting with the tenacity and purposefulness that characterized all his efforts, and he studied hard to improve his skills. He subscribed to a correspondence course in advanced accounting and auditing and read everything he could lay his hands on about those subjects. "I applied myself to my work in the effort to get all of the educational value I could out of it," he wrote.

McGladrey quickly found his assumptions confirmed: public accounting was the right fit for him. "Perhaps it takes a peculiar type of mentality to like public accounting work," he wrote. "I remember one audit I made in Des Moines, which was the first that had been made of that corporation. I had to get out all the musty old records going back twenty years or more on such things as capital stock, surplus, fixed assets, etc. I was given the directors' room all to myself to work in. I had the books piled up on the long table, and was enjoying myself shaping up the financial picture of the past, when I began to get the peculiar sensation one gets when he feels he is being observed. I turned around and there in the doorway stood the president and general manager. He had evidently been looking at me for some time. Finally he said, 'Do you really *like* to do that?' When I assured him I liked it better than any other work I had ever done, he said he didn't see how anyone

Ira McGladrey was known to friends and colleagues as "Mac." 1) McGladrey at the age of 16 in 1899. 2) and 3) As a World War I "doughboy," 1917–1919. 4) With his daughter, Kathleen, in 1925. 5) and 6) Enjoying the great outdoors in the early 1940s.

Chapter 1: Made in the Midwest (1926-1977)

could. I told him that possibly one had to be a little touched in the head to like it. He was the salesman type and I suppose he did think anyone had to be a little nutty to enjoy work of that kind."

About a year after he started work, the Hawthorne & Widdup accounting practice was sold, and McGladrey went job hunting again. This time his search led him to Billings, Prouty and Tompkins, a firm headquartered in Des Moines, with branch offices in nearby Waterloo, Davenport, and Cedar Rapids. McGladrey was put in charge as the manager of the Cedar Rapids office, which consisted of a single room in the Cedar Rapids Savings Bank Building, on October 1, 1920. He managed that office for six years, during which time he passed the Uniform CPA Examination and was made a partner in the firm.

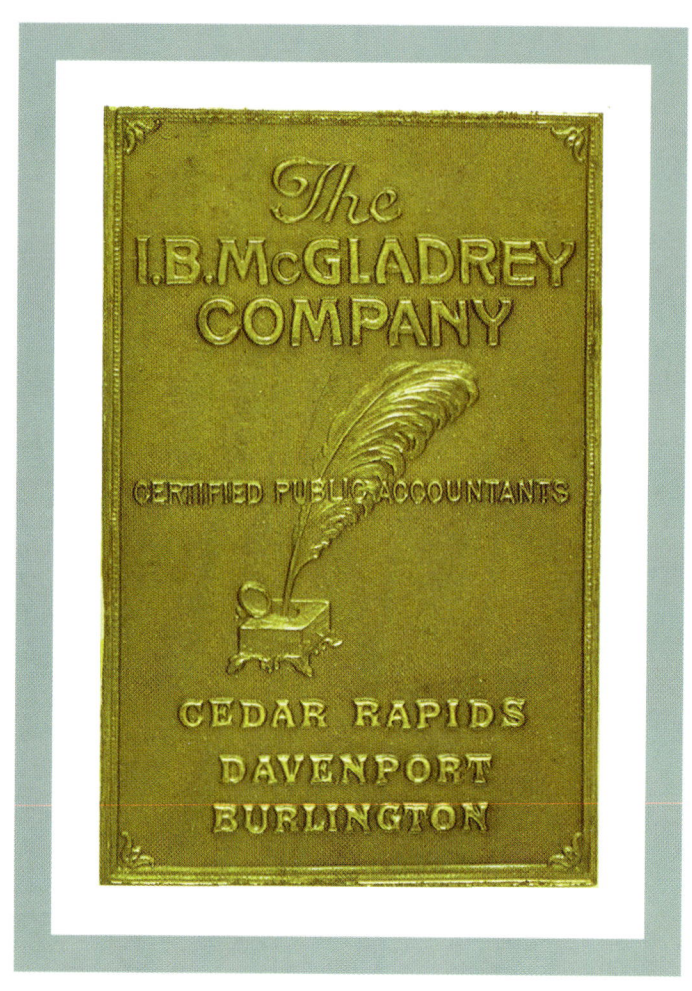

In 1926, when Ira was 43 years old, the firm reorganized. C. B. Tompkins, who had started the Cedar Rapids office, left the firm, and the remaining partners offered to sell that office to McGladrey—under whose leadership Cedar Rapids had grown into a thriving, seven-person operation. Billings and Prouty candidly admitted there was nothing to stop him from simply taking over the practice without paying anything for it. "I said this was doubtless true, but I had no intention of doing so," McGladrey wrote. He agreed to pay $7,500 for the "goodwill" that made the practice viable as well as purchase the physical assets of the office. He also bought the firm's one-man practice at Davenport for an additional $500, and on June 1, 1926, the I. B. McGladrey Company was born.

The cover of the first partners' book

While the new business didn't necessarily thrive, it did well enough that in 1928, McGladrey established a small new office in Burlington, Iowa, "'cold turkey,' so to speak," he recalled upon the twenty-fifth anniversary of his entry into the profession. "We began with no clients and no particular entrée except some help from Mr. Carver of Muscatine. We never afterward have established an office in this way and never expect to do so again. But the office soon was on a prosperous basis and has been a very satisfactory addition to our practice."

Audit and Client Service: The Firm's Foundation

Audit was the firm's first line of business when the I. B. McGladrey Company was formed in 1926 and its primary service for many years after. Ira McGladrey himself set the firm's standard for professional excellence in the business. He was a prime mover in making Iowa one of the first states to adopt regulatory accounting legislation. In the 1940s, McGladrey's decision to issue straightforward opinions on financial reports pushed the firm to the forefront of its profession, and in 1949 he pursued and won adoption of "Statement 23" by the American Institute of Certified Public Accoutants. While his leadership impacted the wider field of public accounting, McGladrey never lost sight of the most important entities his firm's auditors had to impact: their clients.

"Auditing was really a great training ground for me and our people on how businesses operate," said former managing partner Bill Travis, who began working as an auditor for McGladrey predecessor Broeker Hendrickson in 1975. "You got to work very closely with a terrific client and smart entrepreneurs and chief financial officers and just learned a lot about the world of business, and that remains true today." While the practice has changed over the years, Travis said, "I think the fundamentals of being successful are the same. You have to be technically very good as it relates to professional standards and the firm-audit methodology, and you have to be a good client server, which means you have to understand your client really well . . . You have to be a great listener, and you have to demonstrate a high degree of care and concern for your customer. Somebody told me once that clients won't care about you until you demonstrate that you care about them."

Their work as auditors allowed McGladrey professionals to develop a relationship with their clients that was "family advisory—all things business and sometimes things personal, right down to advice on, 'How do I deal with my problem child?' or 'What do you think I should do to solve this problem within my family?'" said Tom Siders, who joined McGladrey in 1975. "You develop a counselor relationship with a client on financial matters, and they have a tendency to come to you for advice on other matters. I had a client call me at 6:30 one Sunday morning. He was unable to sleep all night, because he was worried about the safety of his deposits in a local bank. His balance was over the FDIC limit and he had been hearing rumors the bank was in financial trouble. So I spent some time on a Sunday morning, talking him off the ledge. The people who are really good at it stay in public accounting, in my opinion, like the variety. They like solving problems, they enjoy helping businesses, and they enjoy helping the people who have businesses."

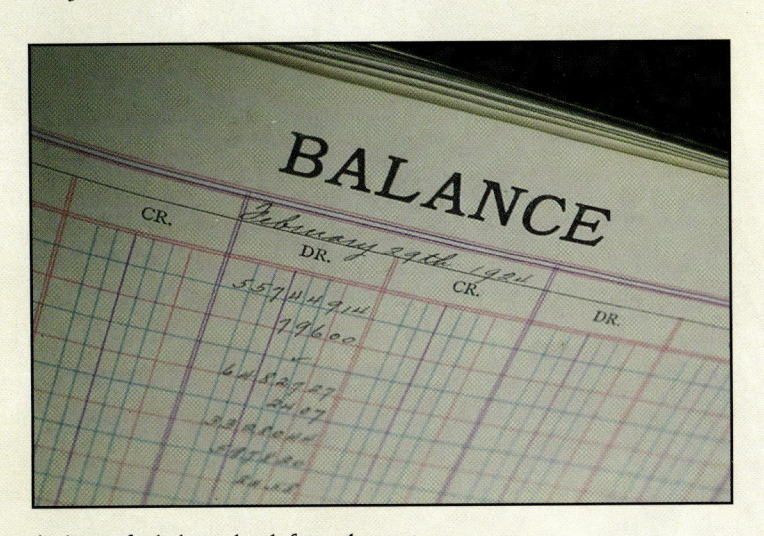

A sheet of a balance book from the past

Chapter 1: Made in the Midwest (1926-1977)

NOT-SO-DEPRESSING TIMES

The stock market crash of 1929 had a tremendous effect on the profession of public accounting. Accountants were given a new mandate to pore over the books of public companies to ensure that the financial records accurately reflected their health. Certified public accountants quickly gained status as a profession and were respected for their financial acumen and moral leadership as a hedge against unscrupulous companies who might try to hoodwink an unsuspecting public.

During the Great Depression, McGladrey managed to keep his business afloat with new work from the State of Iowa, auditing government institutions and agencies. As a result, not only did he not have to lay off workers, he was able to keep giving them raises—albeit modest ones—and even hiring new employees. "The staff continued to grow, especially at Cedar Rapids, and by 1930 the staff room became so unbearably crowded that we had to remodel the offices," McGladrey recalled. "Sufficient additional space was taken on to give everyone plenty of room, we thought."

Among the new hires were two recent University of Iowa graduates: George H. Hansen, who spent six months as a door-to-door women's hosiery salesman before joining McGladrey in November 1930, and Keith W. Dunn, who had been employed by three different Chicago public accounting firms before starting work at McGladrey in the spring of 1931.

During the 1930s, the firm had no formal "time-off program," Hansen recalled in his memoirs. "Mr. McGladrey did, however, tolerate, if not encourage, a delightful substitute. On the slow days, which were many between March 15 and

The foreword McGladrey wrote for the first partners' book

January 1, the lunch hour often lasted at least until two o'clock, sometimes longer. This afforded time for everyone in the office to play cards, generally 'pitch' or Hi-Lo Jack and Game. The stakes were high, five cents a game or double if you were 'schneidered.' Mr. McGladrey played too and had as much fun as staff members, even though his pleasure must have been dampened by the thought that we were all on his payroll."

In 1933 the I. B. McGladrey Company acquired its fourth office when the only accountant practicing in Iowa City, Iowa, passed away. "[H]is widow sold us all of the goodwill that could be salvaged. It was a very poor time to start an office, and we had a lot of trouble keeping it going, but finally it developed into a reasonably profitable, small-sized office," wrote McGladrey.

George Hansen was transferred to Davenport on June 1, 1934, and a year later he was in charge of his own one-man operation. "To say that I started out as an apprehensive branch manager is an understatement," he wrote. "In June 1935 I was 25 years old and was afraid that the few clients we did have would not accept a 'kid bookkeeper.' This fear was not exactly groundless. An early happening was the loss of our one big client. However, Mr. McGladrey gave all the support he could to his fledging manager. He even went so far as to make him a partner . . . I'm sure the triggering factor was Mr. McGladrey's knowledge that I would need all the status possible to gain any kind of client acceptance."

Milestones for a Young Accountant

In his memoirs, Practicing Public Accounting with McGladrey, Hansen, Dunn & Company 1930 to 1975, *George Hansen chronicled many of the landmark moments of his career.*

Starting work: "I had my first argument with Mr. McGladrey even before starting to work. After quitting Real Silk [Hosiery Mills, for whom he worked briefly as a door-to-door salesman] and getting ready to move to Cedar Rapids, I got a letter asking me to defer my starting date from November 1 to December 1. Presumably Mr. McGladrey's Scotch instinct told him there was no need to waste $125 [Hansen's monthly salary]. We reached a compromise and I actually began to work on November 16, 1930."

First client: "The first client I remember working for was a small Cedar Rapids company for which our firm made up monthly statements. After I had proudly delivered my first report to this client, the owner looked it over for a few minutes and then asked a question that I'll never forget: 'Where do I find out how much I made?'"

First busy season: "My first busy season in public accounting was both interesting and demanding. Between January 1 and March 15 everyone worked a seven-day work-week, including evenings, except on Saturday and Sunday . . . It might be worth noting that during most of the 1930s The I. B. McGladrey Company had no adding machines except two broken-down comptometers. Mr. McGladrey felt that anyone claiming to be an 'expert' accountant should surely be able to add and subtract. In fact, fast mental dexterity with arithmetic was a good way to impress clients."

Passing the Uniform CPA Examination: "The great day came in July [1933] when I got the news that I had passed the examination. As was the custom for such occasions, my wife Helen and I promptly hosted a party for all of the people in Cedar Rapids office and their spouses, from Mr. McGladrey on down. The budget suffered, but it was worth it!"

Becoming a partner: "...Keith Dunn and George Hansen each became equal, although very junior, partners on June 1, 1935, at the ripe age of 25 years. (Incidentally, my ego took a little beating when I first learned that Keith Dunn had graduated from the University of Iowa when he was still 19 years old. I thought I had done quite well to get through before my 21st birthday.")

Chapter 1: Made in the Midwest (1926-1977)

Tax: The First Specialty

McGladrey's first tax "specialist" was Keith Dunn, hired in 1931. When Dunn took a leave of absence following World War II, the firm sorely needed a replacement for its tax expert. It was fortunate in being able to hire former IRS employee Roy E. Barnes. "At first, not all Cedar Rapids clients were happy about this move," George Hansen wrote in his memoirs. "A familiar question was, 'What the devil are you doing, hiring that S.O.B.?' It seems that quite a few clients had paid tax assessments as a result of Mr. Barnes' efforts.

Tax returns had to be filled out by hand.

Mr. McGladrey had a very pat answer. It was, 'If you can't lick 'em, jine [join] 'em.'"

Barnes was very smart, said Ivan Bull. "If you had a problem and tried to tell him about it, he'd say, 'Here's the problem—not the one you are telling me about.' So he'd redefine the problem and then solve it for you." While McGladrey's tax man was based in the Cedar Rapids, Iowa, office, he "rode the circuit," spending time in the firm's other practice locations to offer advice and help out when needed.

Barnes was an "institution in the firm," said Jack Wahlig, who joined the firm in 1954. "When I went to Dubuque [to open a new office], I had about three years of experience, and looking back, I probably didn't have enough experience to do what I did. Roy was very worried about me giving tax advice, and so when I went there he gave me a roll of dimes and said, 'If anybody asks you a tax question, you just excuse yourself for a while, get to a pay phone, and call me, and I'll tell you what the answer is,'" laughed Wahlig. "He was tremendous support for me."

When additional specialists were added, Barnes became the firm's first tax coordinator. He was succeeded in the mid-1960s by Paul Cremer, who was based in the Des Moines office. Cremer was instrumental in hiring a large number of tax specialists. "Tax really evolved from being something that was in some sense a support function for the audit practice," said Kimpa Moss, who joined McGladrey in 1986 in Illinois as a senior tax accountant. In the past, the audit partners typically had the primary contact with a client and the primary responsibility for the client engagement, she said. "Over the course of the last twenty years, we've really evolved where tax has a much more leading role in the client relationship and a more direct role in the client relationship." Specialization has allowed the firm to deliver deeper advice, Moss said. The separation of audit and tax into two separate functions was a necessity. "They're separate functions because nobody could hold in their head all the requirements for both," said Moss.

```
                        INTER-OFFICE
                       December 16, 1966                    COPY


    CENTRAL OFFICE

    TO:   IVAN BULL

    IN RE:  BUDGET FOR CONTINUING EDUCATION FOR TAX MEN


    Dear Ivan:

    This estimated budget is for the fiscal year beginning February 1, 1967 for the
    12 tax men of our organization.

    With regard to external training, I estimate 5 days for each, or a total of 480
    hours.  For internal training, I estimate 4 days for each in attending seminars,
    with an additional 12 hours preparatory time.  This results in a total of 528
    hours.

    I estimate the expense as follows:

         External training:
              Travel, Hotel & meals  $300 per man            $ 3,600
              Registrations          $150 per man              1,800

         Internal training:
              Travel, hotel & meals  $100 per man              1,200
                        Total estimated expenditures         $ 6,600


                                            Sincerely yours,

                                            CEDAR RAPIDS OFFICE


                                            Roy E. Barnes

    REB:wk
```

By 1967 McGladrey had twelve "tax men" on staff.

In fact, both Hansen and Dunn were made partners on June 1, 1935–Hansen in the Davenport office and Dunn in Cedar Rapids. "The fact that I was a partner in the Davenport office and Keith Dunn a partner in the Cedar Rapids office did not mean that we shared directly in the profits of those offices. Mr. McGladrey was a firm believer in the 'one-firm' concept. When I became a partner, I lost my arrangement to share in the earnings of the Davenport office. Mr. McGladrey wanted each of his two partners to be equally interested in the success of all offices." Four years later, the firm's name changed to McGladrey, Hansen, Dunn & Company, the name it would keep for the next forty years. "Mr. McGladrey had apparently decided that his two young partners were going to make it," Hansen said.

WAR BRINGS CHANGE

The nation's entry into World War II meant more changes for the firm. Many clients and employees, including Ira McGladrey himself, were called to military service. Ira had been a reserve officer since World War I and was called up for active duty at the age of 59. "In what may be considered the typical army approach, Major McGladrey was not given a financial assignment, even though there was an overwhelming need for competent financial men," reported Hansen. "Instead, he was assigned to the Army Transport Service, an area in which he had little or no background. Fortunately, for both our firm and for Mr. McGladrey, when his unit was scheduled abroad, he could not pass the physical examination and was permitted to return to civilian life."

McGladrey was called up in June 1942 and discharged in August 1943. During his absence, Hansen and Dunn gave up most of their direct client-service activity to manage the practice. Dunn assumed primary responsibility for auditing, accounting, and tax service, as well as taking over Ira's job of reviewing all reports issued by the firm, along with supporting work papers. Hansen spent the bulk of his time on practice administration, including recruiting and other personnel matters, supervision and guidance of the operating offices, and some consultation with partners, staff, and clients on accounting, auditing, and tax matters. "Keith Dunn and I by no means completely segregated our jobs. I helped out in his area and he in mine," Hansen said.

> *Four years later, the firm's name changed to McGladrey, Hansen, Dunn & Company, the name it would keep for the next forty years. "Mr. McGladrey had apparently decided that his two young partners were going to make it," George Hansen said.*

When McGladrey returned to the firm, he resumed most of the review responsibility, but neither Hansen nor Dunn ever returned to handling substantial client services. "The practice had grown to such an extent that it seemed that we could make our best contribution by remaining as executive partners. The three of us operated pretty much as a team, with Mr. McGladrey being the 'most equal' among equals," Hansen wrote. "We consulted with each other on all aspects of the practice. Mr. McGladrey devoted most of his time to his primary interests, accounting and reporting. Keith Dunn as fully occupied with tax problems, and I continued to spend most of my time on administrative matters . . . Mr. McGladrey was the report department, Keith Dunn the tax department, and I, more or less, the Central Office."

World War II had dramatically altered the practice of public account-

George Hansen, Keith Dunn, and Ira B. McGladrey in 1945

ing. "The industrial mobilization necessary to supply war materiel and the drastic increase in income taxes necessary to pay their costs boomed the demand for accounting services. At the same time, the people needed to supply those services were harder and harder to come by. The change in the personnel situation from one of plenty to one of scarcity occurred almost overnight," wrote Hansen. To stay competitive, McGladrey added nearly a dozen schools to its former two-school recruiting schedule. "The problem was not only to hire people, but to keep those we had," Hansen said—which the firm did in part by making some of its best qualified staff men partners.

Chapter 1: Made in the Midwest (1926-1977)

Time for a Party

```
                    PARTY EXPENSES
        PRIZES:
        Jewel case-lady's Prize         $4.06
        4 golf balls-man's prize         3.88
        Set of coasters                  1.28
        Clothes brush                    1.02
        Chocolate cigarettes              .20
        Easter eggs                       .15
        Key chain                         .26
        Ash trays (2)                    1.02
                    Paid by Marcia              $11.87
        Pen-pencil set                   1.02
        Handcuffs                         .26
        Car                               .10
                    Paid by Mary                  1.38
        Gun                               .26
                    Paid by Dorothea               .26
        Double deck of cards             1.53
        Puzzle                           1.02
        Matches                          1.02
        Jack pot game                    1.02    4.59*
            Total cost of prizes                       $18.10
        Wrapping paper and string
                    Paid by Marcia            .31
                    Paid by Mary              .26      .57
                                                    $18.67
Other Expenses:
    Name tags:
        Construction paper -Paid by Mary    .16
          "            "      "   Marcia    .31       .47
        Pins                                          .10
        Score pads                                    .21
        Tip for bartender                            3.00
                                           Eugene 1.00    4.00
        Cigarettes                                   5.40
        Nuts and candy                               2.55
        Ray Long (Check was short)                   5.00
        Check girl(Had allowed
            $1.00 but paid 2.00)                     1.00   18.73
*Charged at Killian's                                      $37.40
```

Copy of a receipt for the party

Spring 1946. The war was over, and with the men of McGladrey, Hansen, Dunn & Company back from the front and behind their desks, Ira McGladrey threw a party to celebrate. He rented the grand ballroom of the swank Roosevelt Hotel in downtown Cedar Rapids to host a formal dinner for the entire firm, thanking everyone who worked for him for their hard work and sacrifice during the just-completed busy season. No expense was spared: McGladrey's spread featured only the choicest prime steaks and the best vintage wines. On the appointed evening in April, employees of the offices in Burlington, Davenport, Iowa City, and Keokuk drove all the way to Cedar Rapids for the event, the men wearing their best suits, the women their most elegant dresses— some even wearing long, white gloves.

Ira B. McGladrey and his wife, Bernice, sit at the head of the table during the 1946 firm-wide party at the Roosevelt Hotel in Cedar Rapids. George and Helen Hansen sit to their right; Keith and Peg Dunn sit to their left.

Chapter 1: Made in the Midwest (1926-1977)

When the war ended, Keith Dunn took a leave of absence to become an executive vice president of one of the firm's bigger clients. Although he remained a partner in McGladrey, Hansen, Dunn & Company and continued to consult with Ira McGladrey and George Hansen on a fairly regular basis, his departure from the day-to-day business meant the firm needed someone to replace his tax expertise. With the arrival of Roy E. Barnes, a former Internal Revenue Service employee, the firm established its own tax department.

Dunn's leave of absence also resulted in a restructuring of the partnership organization, in which recognition of partnership goodwill superseded the one-firm concept. The change was designed to encourage growth by giving the partners in each practice substantial control over the operation of their offices and tying their income closely with office results. Separate partnerships were formed to operate each McGladrey office, and the original McGladrey, Hansen, Dunn & Company partnership then became a holding company. Some earnings were allocated to goodwill ownership, instituting the Average Annual Volume (AAV) concept.

McGladrey, Hansen, Dunn & Company continued growing. It had purchased its first firm, Allison and Associates, with offices in Davenport and Omaha, in 1939. Soon other firms were purchased, and new offices opened, in Des Moines and Janesville, Wisconsin. As McGladrey acquired clients in a wider territory, the firm often sent one of its younger men to a new area to establish a foothold. Offices were opened in Clinton, Iowa, in 1947 by Jim Cover; Keokuk, Iowa, in 1949 by Charlie Cole; and Rock Island, Illinois, in 1950 by Ivan O. Bull. "The establishment of these three offices also provided places for capable young accountants in our organization where they could develop their talents and show what they could do," wrote Ira McGladrey. "There were no vacancies in existing partnerships, and these men had the natural ability and had obtained the experience to entitle them to advancement. Either we opened new offices or we eventually lost such men." The opening of Rock Island brought the total number of operating offices to ten.

Ira McGladrey slowly began to pull back from the firm as he edged closer to retirement. In 1945, when he was 62, he separated the firm's executive division from its client service office and became the head of the former, reluctantly ending his work with clients. He also spent more of his time in attempts to reform the accounting industry, making it more accountable to clients.

> "The establishment of these three offices also provided places for capable young accountants in our organization where they could develop their talents and show what they could do," wrote Ira McGladrey.

A Legacy to the Accounting Industry

Throughout his career in public accounting, Ira McGladrey was a leader in the profession at both the state and national levels. While McGladrey was building his young firm, he was also building a name for himself within the state of Iowa and the accounting profession. He was elected president of the Iowa Society of Certified Public Accountants in 1928. That winter was "made memorable to Iowa Accountants by the legislative battle over the Regulatory Accountancy Act," wrote McGladrey, who led the society to pass a bill outlining an examination for public accountants who had been in practice for seven years or more at the effective date. "Under this law all practicing public accountants were registered by the Iowa Board of Accountancy, and as I was appointed a member of that Board and was elected secretary and treasurer, most of the chores in that connection fell on me."

Throughout his career, McGladrey frequently traveled from Cedar Rapids to serve as a guest lecturer at University of Iowa business and accounting classes. He also was instrumental in the merger of the American Society of CPAs and the American Institute of Accountants. He first proposed such a merger in 1933 to little notice, but he continued to push until convincing enough members of both groups to form a single professional group; the American Institute of Certified Public Accountants (AICPA) was created in 1936.

Perhaps his greatest contribution to the profession came in the 1940s, when McGladrey launched a one-man crusade to make CPAs assume a greater degree of responsibility for their audits. Though a substantial body of accepted auditing practice had been developed, McGladrey found that 80 to 90 percent of all auditors' reports included no opinion, and professional standards didn't require auditors to state why no opinion was offered. In 1946 he waged his first attack with an article published in the Journal of Accountancy *titled "What is the Accountant's Proper Responsibility?" He advocated that the entire profession adopt the policy his firm was in the process of implementing, which was, when issuing a financial statement, to either express an unqualified opinion or admit that not enough is known about the financial statements to form an opinion and outline why.*

McGladrey, Hansen, Dunn & Company—particularly the Davenport office—served as a guinea pig for the new policy. "Although we had no professional backing on which to stand, most of our clients liked our new approach and many of the knowledgeable ones said they couldn't understand why accountants hadn't done this before," George Hansen wrote. "We didn't lose a single client; in fact, our volume increased substantially because several clients who had previously 'gotten by' decided to have an opinion audit."

For three years McGladrey wrote letters and articles, made speeches, and traveled the country lobbying for corrective reform. His work finally paid off in 1949 when the American Institute of Accountants adopted "Statement 23," or the Fourth Standard of Reporting of the generally accepted auditing standards, which all AICPA members still follow today.

For many years Ira McGladrey led a campaign to eliminate deceptive and inconclusive information found in many audit reports throughout the profession, and in 1949 the American Institute of Certified Public Accountants adopted Statement 23, requiring public auditors to express or disclaim an opinion on financial statements written in the report. Just a few months after this victory, upon returning from a professional ethics committee meeting in New York, McGladrey discovered early symptoms of prostate cancer. He chose to reveal the diagnosis to no one except his closest relatives and business partners. "I would be inclined to believe that my reasons were twofold," he wrote in his memoirs. "I did not think it would be desirable for business reasons, and I hated to think of the kind of pity it would elicit from my friends and acquaintances."

"Although his illness and its treatment required Mr. McGladrey to work less and less, he didn't quit until the very end," said Hansen. "He continued to review some reports and work papers at home until such work was made impossible by physical weakness and pain." Ira McGladrey died on February 19, 1952, five days before his 69th birthday. In the rapidly changing public accounting profession, few men's names endure beyond their years. Today, more than half a century after his death, the firm founded by Ira McGladrey still bears both his name and his dedication to the improvement of the profession.

NEW LEADERSHIP

Upon McGladrey's death, Keith Dunn ended his leave of absence and with Hansen became an equal owner in the holding company partnership, with Dunn overseeing the Cedar Rapids practice and Hansen in charge at Davenport. The two men were "as different as night and day," said Jack Wahlig, who joined the firm in 1954. "George was a rough-hewn kind of guy. It isn't too hard to picture George in a street fight. Keith Dunn, on the other hand, was the ultimate sophisticate: debonair, interested in every topic in the world. They were as much different as any two people could be, but they were both good for the firm. I think they respected each other and respected each other's differences. Of the two, I think George Hansen had a much greater impact on the firm."

George Hansen took over as managing partner and made growth one of his priorities, acquiring still more offices throughout Iowa and the Midwest, and McGladrey began to show more of a profit. Under Hansen's leadership, the firm adopted a "model corporation report," which used a single

> *"George Hansen used to say, 'Give 'em some Green Stamps,'" recalled Jack Wahlig. "What he meant was, give them something extra. They're paying for the audit, they're paying for tax work, but give them a bonus, give them suggestions."*

McGladrey: Beyond the Balance Sheet, 1926-2008

report style to replace the many different styles of reports that accountants used for different clients. The new reports helped the firm grow because they were recognized by clients and potential clients, and better accepted, and they saved time because accountants needed to learn to complete and read only a single report form. The firm also started what was called the "POP" program. The acronym "POP" stands for Planned Objectives and Procedures. This system created a year-round planning program to collect client files to reduce work during the busy season, as well as reduce fraud. Both the model corporation report and POP files system became the basis for McGladrey's accounting manuals and were later adopted by many other accounting firms.

McGladrey's relationships with its clients, however, remained the primary focus of its service lines. The majority of the firm's clients were small, independent businesses and individuals needing help with income tax returns, and the accountants were determined to deliver service above and beyond what was required. "George Hansen used to say, 'Give 'em some Green Stamps,'" recalled Jack Wahlig. "What he meant was, give them something extra. They're paying for the audit, they're paying for tax work, but give them a bonus, give them suggestions. Give them something that will help them be more profitable. So my partners and I grew up in an environment where just doing the audit and just doing the tax work wasn't enough; we had to try to 'add value' before that phrase was ever coined."

George Hansen

Over time, the firm's work began to be more complicated due to changes in the tax law and the regulation of audit. "As business became more complicated, our services became more complicated," said Ivan Bull. McGladrey performed its first public audit in 1954 for supermarket chain Eagle Food Centers, under the guidance of John Hoyt. Eagle was already a McGladrey client when it decided to go public. "Back then, if you went to one of the major underwriters, they would say, 'We want you to change CPA firms to a Big 8 firm,'" said Wahlig.

Chapter 1: Made in the Midwest (1926-1977)

"Our client, Dick Waxenberg, who was the president of Eagle Food, said, 'Gee, you fellas misunderstood me. I'm looking for an underwriter. I've already got a good CPA firm.' He convinced Merrill Lynch that McGladrey was a good firm and totally capable of taking him public. Merrill Lynch finally agreed but said that McGladrey had to hire Arthur Andersen, which was then the premier CPA firm in the country, to look over its shoulder." Arthur Andersen proved "a good big brother to us" and the audit was a success. Hoyt subsequently became McGladrey's first Securities and Exchange Commission (SEC) coordinator and a leader in SEC-related work.

When Keith Dunn retired, on November 1, 1960, Leo E. Burger and Ivan Bull became, along with Hansen, the firm's executive partners. Burger had first joined McGladrey in 1942; shortly thereafter he was called back into the U.S. Navy but returned to the Cedar Rapids office following the war. Bull, also a World War II veteran, started working in the firm's Iowa City office while still an undergraduate accounting student at the University of Iowa and was hired full-time upon his graduation in 1947; he spent three years in Davenport before being placed in charge of the Rock Island office when it was opened in 1950. Upon Dunn's retirement, Hansen moved the central office from Cedar Rapids to Davenport, a move that, he reported, "was quite easy": "All that had to be moved was the accounting department, which at the time consisted of one person."

In 1964, spearheaded by Ivan Bull, McGladrey returned to a one-firm concept, giving more control to the managing partner and newly created board of directors and reducing both office provincialism and inter-office competition. McGladrey began the transformation from a collection of individual offices—"a loose confederation," as many described it—

Ivan Bull, born on an Iowa farm in 1924, served two and a half years in the infantry during World War II. Upon graduating from the University of Iowa in 1947, he started working with McGladrey, Hansen, Dunn & Company. He was promoted to partner in 1951 and served as managing partner from 1966 to 1982. Bull served as chairman of the AICPA in 1976. Ivan was also one of the original trustees of the Financial Accounting Foundation, which was the sponsoring organization of the Financial Accounting Standards Board which has been responsible for U.S. accounting standard for the past 35 years. Following his retirement from the firm in 1982, Bull returned to school to earn his Ph.D. and subsequently taught at the University of Illinois.

to one firm. It was a process that took several years to complete.

"A lot of people have had impact on the firm, but I think Ivan had *the* critical impact on the firm," said Wahlig. "When I joined the firm, we had an awful lot of local office autonomy . . . You pretty much focused on your own office because that's where you ate. Ivan had the idea that we needed to be one firm. We needed to all share the good and the bad that happened everyplace in the firm, and we should have just as much interest in seeing that another office has the resources it needs to serve its clients well as our own office . . . It sounds kind of easy—it sounds like we all should have said 'yes'—but it was a tough sell to a bunch of hard-headed accountants who were used to, 'I eat what I kill.'"

Bull continued to advocate for a one-firm sentiment during his term as managing partner, which began when George Hansen retired in 1966. Bull was assisted by David F. Wentworth, who served as the firm's executive partner. Like Bull, Wentworth was an AICPA Sells silver-medal award winner for receiving the second-highest grade of anyone taking the same Uniform CPA Examination in the United States; he had joined McGladrey in 1948, working primarily in the Davenport office. Bull also was supported by Leo Burger, who carried principal responsibility for accounting, auditing, and reporting policies until 1972.

Under its new management, McGladrey, Hansen, Dunn & Company grew "faster than ever, in every way," a recently retired Hansen observed. Between 1966 and 1975, the number of operating offices nearly doubled, and the number of people serving in those locations nearly tripled. New products and services were being created, and the quality of all services was enhanced by both improved and expanded personnel employment and training programs and by added emphasis on quality control. Expansion in size coupled with the one-firm structure allowed McGladrey to begin to offer clients increased specialization, starting with management consulting, and to begin looking outside the Midwest for its clientele. Mergers in Wyoming in 1972 and California and Nevada in 1977 brought in offices in new areas, and McGladrey began to explore the possibility of expanding further.

Longtime Client: Augustana College

The Augustana College and Seminary in Rock Island, Illinois, was a small Lutheran liberal arts college with a handful of buildings on a beautiful leafy campus and an outstanding academic heritage when the I. B. McGladrey Co. started keeping its accounts in the 1930s. Much has changed at "Augie" since then, but a few things have not: the campus remains beautiful, its outstanding academic record continues, and McGladrey & Pullen still does its accounting work.

"I have great confidence in your ongoing expertise," said Paul Pearson, Augie's chief business and financial officer. "Just knowing you're there is helpful." Bob Larsen, managing director, Moline, and Dale Dollenbacher, senior manager, Davenport, are the college's client service coordinators. The firm provides historical audit and business advisory services, consulting services, and meets regularly with the college's financial team to discuss various issues. Larsen and Dollenbacher said working for a college client is considerably different than working for a corporate client because a college's mission is not to turn a profit but to educate young people and prepare them for life. "In working with Augustana, it's important we understand its mission and plan what we do and bring to the table around that," said Dollenbacher. Larsen said he enjoys the uniqueness of working with a college client. "There's always a new experience every year," he said.

Diane McNulty: A McGladrey Pioneer

Mason City tax partner Diane McNulty hard at work.

Diane McNulty was an unusual sight around McGladrey, Hansen and Dunn's Mason City office when she was hired in August 1966. She was a woman, and she did accounting work.

It wasn't unusual for women to work for the firm in those days, even going back to its founding. But most worked as secretaries, receptionists, and in other office administrative jobs that women were largely confined to in American business before the 1960s. Only a few were members of the firm's professional staff, and even then they worked mostly as bookkeepers or paraprofessionals. None were CPAs.

McNulty had earned a bachelor of science degree in business administration from Drake University (where she was the only woman accounting major in her class) and worked in private accounting for two years before joining McGladrey. Yet in the early years she was expected to not only be an accountant, but also do what was considered the "women's work" around the office, answering phones and making coffee. "Then I took the CPA exam and passed it the first time; then they had to put me on the professional staff full-time." When she received her CPA certificate in 1968, McNulty was one of only five women in the state of Iowa to hold the certificate and license who worked in the profession. "That's how much the profession has changed, and all for the better," she said.

For the most part, McNulty said her trailblazing was not difficult. "Mason City was a pretty laid-back office," she said. "Being a woman and a CPA might have been difficult in a bigger office, but I had good working relationships with everyone. The clients didn't care, either. Once they realized I could do the work, the fact that I was a woman didn't bother them. I guess I always felt I was well accepted by clients, but coming from a small community in Iowa, it might have been easier."

When McNulty was made a partner in 1976, she was the first woman voted to be a partner in the firm's history. At her first partners' meeting, the "fellas," as McNulty affectionately referred to her male cohorts, took a run at testing her mettle. "They were very cordial to me, but they would get to telling really raunchy stories in front of me at the meeting. I just sat there very calmly and didn't turn red or get flustered and just accepted it for what it was. After the meeting, I got a nice note in the mail from Ivan Bull [then managing partner of the firm] that said, 'I was so proud of how you handled yourself. Perhaps we won't have to go through all this nonsense again.'

"As far as blazing a path, I always tried to do my best job and do what I loved to do, and the fact that they continued to name women partners to the firm speaks for itself."

Chapter Two

Growth Spurts

(1977-1999)

Moline, Illinois. Elkhart, Indiana. Casper, Wyoming. Fort Dodge, Iowa. Marshalltown, Iowa. Cedar Rapids, Iowa. McGladrey, Hansen, Dunn & Company had found its niche in the country's small-town communities.

"We were the only show in town," said Tom Siders, who started with the firm on January 1, 1975, right out of the University of Iowa. Siders worked as a staff accountant in Cedar Rapids, the original office from which Ira B. McGladrey had started his practice. In the Midwest, McGladrey, Hansen, Dunn & Company was the proverbial big fish in a little pond.

The Big 8 [now the Big 4] had tried and failed to penetrate our marketplace. We were better at serving the closely held businesses, compared to the Big 8. We really knew those clients better. I remember Ivan Bull once said the Big 8 are organized to serve large, publicly held clients, and they have separate divisions to serve smaller businesses. Our firm is organized to serve closely held businesses, and we have a separate group that serves large, publicly owned businesses. It was just that kind of difference. And as we began to expand through merger, we went to places like Peoria, Illinois, and Rockford and Elkhart, Indiana. We didn't go to Houston, Dallas, San Francisco."

For more than fifty years, McGladrey had enjoyed slow, steady success in public accounting, building up practices based on personal relationships and absorbing small, local accounting firms when prudent. By 1977 it had twenty-nine offices

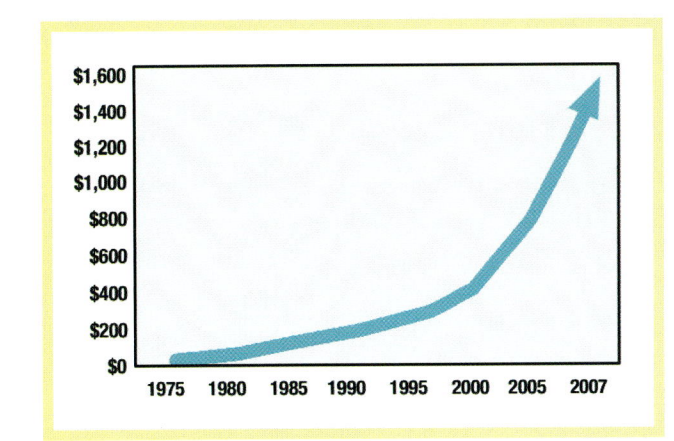

Net Services 1975–2007 (in millions)

"McGladrey had a value-the-firm methodology that absolutely made sense to us," Leroy Martin said.

Becoming a Major Regional Player

Thanks to the professional leadership the firm's partners had always shown, the firm was active in public accounting's professional bodies almost from its inception. Ira McGladrey served on the boards of both the Iowa and American ICPAs and was instrumental in the merger of the American Society of CPAs and the American Institute of Accountants. Leo Burger served on the Accounting Principles Board, a predecessor to the Financial Accounting Standards Board. Managing partner Ivan Bull served as president of the AICPA; he also was one of the original members of the board of trustees to the Financial Accounting Foundation, which formed the Financial Accounting Standards Board. In addition, McGladrey had been a founding partner of Dunwoody Robson McGladrey & Pullen (DRM) International, an affiliation of international accounting and consulting firms whose member firms were located in twenty-one countries and had correspondent firms in an additional twenty countries. All of these involvements served to introduce McGladrey to accounting firms in other parts of the country and, eventually, to potential merger candidates, and the firm began to look seriously at expansion on a larger scale in new territory.

McGladrey's first consideration was A.M. Pullen. & Co. of Richmond, Virginia, a firm with which it had formed a friendship through DRM International. Pullen was recognized for its expertise in many industries, particularly textiles, savings and loans, health care, insurance, local governmental units, and federal agency grants. The firm, based in Richmond, Virginia operated twenty-six offices in seven states from New York to Florida. A merger

Coffee Breaks

"In my early years in Cedar Rapids, employees were provided a morning coffee break," said Tom Siders, who joined the firm as a staff accountant in 1975. *"First, the support staff gathered in the coffee room, for fifteen or twenty minutes. Then the staff had their designated turn for coffee and conversation. Finally, the partners would begin to filter in. I presume the partners were last, by design, to make sure we all got back to work on a timely basis. Regardless, the room cleared out quickly when the partners began to arrive. I used to linger for a while, to listen to stories of early years in the firm and catch the latest news about the local business community. Eventually, one of the partners would give me 'the look' and glance at his wristwatch, which was a signal that I had worn out my welcome."*

would take McGladrey into the Southeast, an area poised for growth, said Tom Horne, executive managing director of McGladrey's Carolina Economic Unit, who started working for A.M. Pullen in 1969 as a staff accountant. Pullen also had a specialty practice that did mutual-fund audits in New York City. "McGladrey was a well-respected Midwestern firm with very little connectivity on the Eastern seaboard. A.M. Pullen was a very well-known Eastern firm–regional–that had very good quality," Horne said. Putting the two together would give both better geographic coverage and increase their overall size, creating a much larger firm with the ability to attract better personnel as well as larger clients.

Serious merger talks with A.M. Pullen began in the late 1970s and were almost consummated. Agreements had been drawn up and the contracts were ready to sign, needing only the approval of each firm's board of directors to be finalized. But just before the McGladrey, Hansen and Dunn board was to consider the deal, a lawsuit was filed against Pullen, and the merger was put on the shelf. While Pullen dealt with the lawsuit, McGladrey shifted gears and focused on a firm closer to home.

Broeker Hendrickson & Co. was headquartered in nearby Minneapolis. McGladrey had become acquainted with the firm through a mutual affiliation with Associated Accounting Firms International, a national organization of small to medium-sized public accounting firms, as well as through participation on the Accounting Principles Board, on which Broeker Hendrickson cofounder Milton Broeker served. The two firms "got to know each other fairly well," said LeRoy Martin, who had begun his accounting career with Broeker Hendrickson in 1962 while still a college student at the University of Minnesota, and believed the two firms would have "compatible" cultures when they came together. "McGladrey had a value-the-firm methodology that absolutely made sense to us," Martin said. "In the old Broeker firm, if you got hit by a truck, kicked out of the firm, or retired, you got nothing, basically. And McGladrey had figured out how to value the firm and create the system to pay off partners: average annual volume."

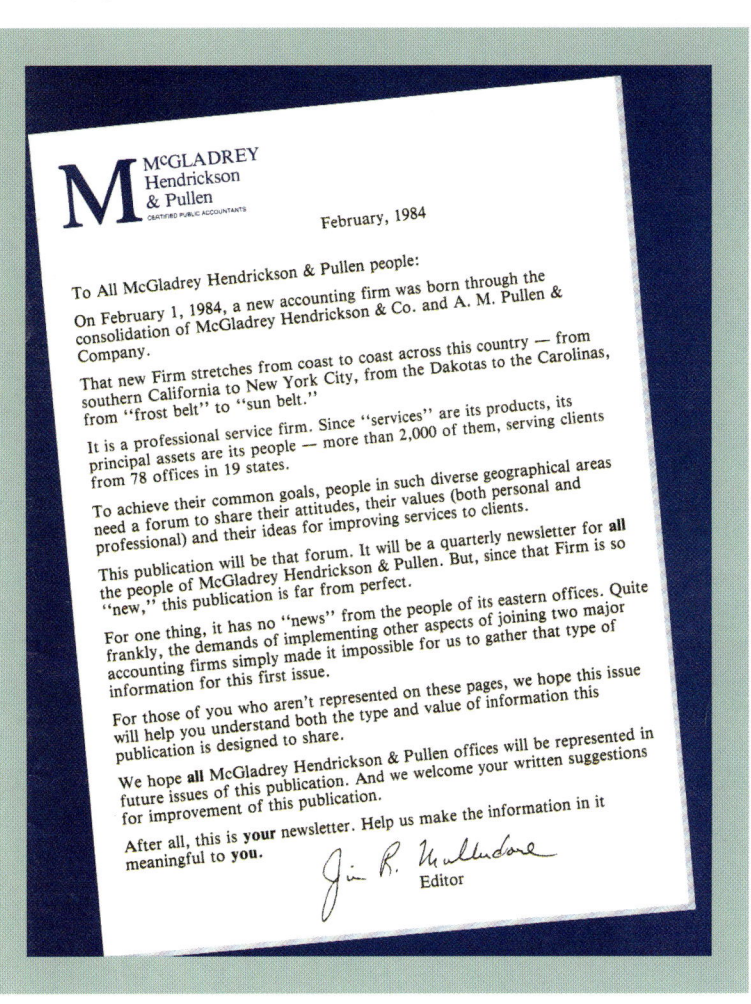

Mpressions, the firm newsletter dedicated to McGladrey & Pullen information, was formed after the merger with A.M. Pullen.

Chapter 2: Growth Spurts (1977-1999)

Broeker Hendrickson & Co.

Broeker Hendrickson & Co. was formed right after World War II when Milton Broeker and Laurence Hendrickson left Arthur Andersen in Minneapolis to start their own practice in 1946. Broeker, a highly regarded auditor on a national level (who would later serve on the Accounting Principles Board), and Hendrickson, a tax specialist, pooled their talents to serve clients in the Twin Cities area.

Broeker was from Minneapolis and Hendrickson from St. Paul, and while they initially operated out of Hendrickson's basement, they settled on the "Midway area" between the two cities for their venture and soon opened their first real office, at Raymond and University avenues in St. Paul. Their partnership proved to be a successful one. By the time Warren Bolmgren joined the firm in 1951, straight out of college following his service in the infantry in Europe during World War II, Broeker Hendrickson operated a second office in Fargo, North Dakota. Bolmgren was interested in working for Broeker Hendrickson in part because he saw the opportunity for a young CPA and a young firm to "grow together," although, he said, he never considered taking a job with the five-year-old company a risk, due largely to the credentials and experience of its founding partners. "Both Milt Broeker and Larry Hendrickson were very capable people," he said.

By the mid-1950s Broeker Hendrickson maintained offices in both Twin Cities downtown areas, with Broeker taking charge of the Minneapolis office and Hendrickson the one in St. Paul. At the time, Bolmgren said, competition existed between the two cities, and there was a financial advantage to be gained by having offices in both sites. It also allowed the firm to be active in both local communities and take advantage of a major source of clients: banks. In Minneapolis the Broeker Hendrickson office was located in the Northwestern Bank building; in St. Paul, the First National Bank building.

Eventually the firm merged with a small but well-established Rochester, Minnesota, firm, sending CPA Jim Rian to incorporate the new personnel into the Broeker Hendrickson fold. This was followed by mergers that took Broeker Hendrickson into Sioux Falls, South Dakota, and Duluth, Minnesota, and the firm continued to expand from there. Milt Broeker got the firm involved with the Associated Accounting Firms International (AAFI), the organization through which it became acquainted with McGladrey, Hansen & Dunn. "We weren't necessarily looking for a merger opportunity, but we got to know McGladrey over a number of years through AAFI, and it just seemed like a good fit," said Bolmgren, who, with the retirement of both Broeker and Hendrickson, became the firm's new managing partner in 1970. By the time of the consolidation with McGladrey in November 1978, Broeker Hendrickson included sixteen offices in five states and had a total staff of nearly 300 people.

Warren Bolmgren, managing partner of Broeker Hendrickson & Co. from 1970 to 1978, was instrumental in the consolidation of that firm with McGladrey, Hansen and Dunn. After the merger, Bolmgren was named McGladrey's Northern Region partner. He also served as president of the Minnesota Society of CPAs in 1974-75.

Larry Hendrickson, Milton Broeker, and Jim Rian

Chapter 2: Growth Spurts (1977-1999)

Blazing a Trail

McGladrey hired its first women accountants during World War II (a time when the firm had "more clients than people," according to former managing partner Ivan Bull) and voted in its first female partner in 1976, but there was still no one to tell Rebecca "Becky" Miller how to dress when she started working as a CPA.

She spent the first two years of her career in a traditional tax role at Arthur Andersen before joining McGladrey in Rochester, Minnesota, in October 1979. "We don't have a standard uniform, so it's always a little more challenging for a woman to find what's appropriate to wear. It took me about two years into the business to figure out what I should wear, and frankly, I modeled myself after the secretary of the managing partner at Arthur Andersen because there were no female CPA models," said Miller. She wore navy striped suits, white shirts, and "little red bow ties." "I can't say I enjoyed it, but all the professional women in the seventies, and even into the early eighties, dressed like that," she said. When the dress code at McGladrey shifted away from a required suit to the slightly more casual sportcoat, Miller made the shift as well, to "the female equivalent of a sports coat," trousers and a blazer.

Miller, who went on to develop experience in the employee-benefit arena, was the fourth woman to make partner in the firm, on February 1, 1984, and takes her role as McGladrey's unofficial women's historian seriously, keeping tabs on the development of female partners and serving as a mentor. "I think in general, we've been very successful," Miller said. The firm has been fabulous. I have never felt at all like I was under any kind of a special scrutiny as a woman in public accounting," she said.

"You build up friendships in your offices, and because you are friends with your coworkers, there is a huge amount of tolerance for your personal needs," said Rebecca Miller, who attended her first partners' meeting in 1984 while pregnant with her daughter Sarah. Two "massive" pieces of pension legislation, the Deficit Reduction Act of 1984 and the Retirement Equity Act of 1984, took effect the following year, she said. "So I brought Sarah into the office. She was so tiny, but there was all this stuff going on, and we didn't have much in the way of infrastructure; national tax was four people at this point in time. And so I brought Sarah into the office. I had to breastfeed her and change her diapers in the office, and if I was on a conference call, my secretary would come in and jiggle her. It's hilarious, but it is representative of some of the best aspects of McGladrey. When we talk about trying to balance work/life, here my choice was to bring my life into my work, and nobody was appalled by that. I did have to make a point of keeping my door closed if the baby was squalling," she laughed.

"I was lucky, and I hope that I've done my fair share to help the other women in the firm."

Miller Testifies Before Congress

Rebecca Miller, Rochester, McGladrey Pension Administration and Consulting Team, testified before the U.S. House of Representatives' Sub-Committee on Employer-Employee Relations in Washington, D.C., Feb. 13, about employee stock ownership retirement plans.

The hearing, one of many Congressional panels looking into the Enron collapse, sought information about ESOPs and how employee retirement plans can be better protected. Miller, an authority on the plans, explained their history and their benefits to employees and employers. "My goal was to emphasize that private company ESOPs are different in two significant aspects, cash flow and value, and Congress must keep that in mind when changing the law," she said. "The sub-committee seemed willing to acknowledge the private company ESOPs served a separate purpose."

Rebecca Miller testifies before a U.S. House of Representatives sub-committee.

One of the congressmen on the sub-committee was Cass Ballenger, a Republican from North Carolina and McGladrey & Pullen client, who praised the Firm during the hearing for the honorable and professional work he's received. **M**

Chapter 2: Growth Spurts (1977-1999)

Evolution of a Name
(1978 through 1987)

Name changes are not new to McGladrey's history. Since 1978 the firm's name has changed three times, twice because of mergers.

For more than forty years, the firm was known as McGladrey, Hansen, Dunn & Company as it grew to twenty-six offices in six Midwestern states.

In 1978 the firm merged with Broeker Hendrickson & Co. to become McGladrey Hendrickson & Co. Broeker Hendrickson & Co., based in the Twin Cities, had sixteen offices in five states. With the merger, McGladrey Hendrickson & Co. served clients in eight states throughout the Midwest.

In 1984 the firm's partners were ready to expand again. A.M. Pullen & Company was a perfect match. Based in North Carolina, A.M. Pullen & Company had twenty-six offices located throughout seven states along the Eastern seaboard. As McGladrey,

Hendrickson & Pullen, the firm's offices extended from the east coast to the west coast and from as far north as Duluth to as far south as Fort Lauderdale.

In late 1987 the firm decided to change the name again, but this time there was no merger involved. On May 1, 1987, the firm officially became known as McGladrey & Pullen.

Although its name has changed over the years, McGladrey's commitment to its clients and to helping them succeed has not changed. As a firm, it still focuses on providing family-owned and closely-held businesses the services they need to grow and prosper.

Like McGladrey, Broeker Hendrickson had been built on a lot of small mergers; it had two offices in North Dakota, two in South Dakota, three in Minnesota, and one in Colorado. All told, the firm brought in sixteen offices in five states and had a total staff of nearly 300 people. "The real reason we came together was we needed to be bigger to be a real force," said Martin. "The world was changing about then, and we needed to be bulked up in order to really do the job."

The deal was completed in November 1978, and McGladrey, Hansen, Dunn and Company and Broeker Hendrickson & Co. came together as equals, Martin said. "The top leadership positions were pretty much split between the two firms." The combined firm of McGladrey, Hendrickson & Co. now served clients from forty-five offices throughout the Midwest.

When the lawsuit against A.M. Pullen was finally settled in the early 1980s, the two sides began talks anew, and the merger was finalized on February 1, 1984. By then, Pullen was about one-third the size of McGladrey Hendrickson & Co., with about 600 employees working from twenty-four offices in seven states. The post-merger firm took the name McGladrey Hendrickson & Pullen, but that many syllables soon proved difficult to pronounce in quick succession and the name was shortened to McGladrey & Pullen in 1987.

Before merging with Broeker Hendrickson and A.M. Pullen, McGladrey was a "small-town firm," said former managing partner Mark Scally, who started with McGladrey in 1971. It emerged from the transactions with new territory and clients, ready to establish itself as a bona fide large regional player. "It was exciting for everyone because the firm was getting bigger, and everyone looked at that as creating more opportunities for everyone," said Siders. "It also helped serve clients better. A bigger organization means more capabilities, perhaps more specialists or experts, and therefore better client service."

GROWING PAINS

Once the deals were done, the firm got down to the business of incorporating its new members, and the transitions were not without considerable growing pains. Despite many similarities between the firms, there were inevitably adjustments that needed to occur—a settling-out process that has to take place, a blending of cultures and procedures and management— "although often that was a lot more about one market versus another as opposed to one firm versus the other," said Horne.

A.M. Pullen & Co.

While the I. B. McGladrey Co., established in 1926, is considered the corporate predecessor to McGladrey & Pullen, the former A.M. Pullen & Co. actually predates it by eighteen years.

Founded in 1908 in Richmond, Virginia, it was first known as Wilson and Pullen, after its founders George Wilson and Alfred Marvin (A.M.) Pullen. Wilson, the office manager for a local shoe company, and Pullen, an associate, ventured from the relative security of their company jobs to establish their own accounting firm. Since neither of them had any real accounting experience, it was a risky venture. But the profession was young: when A. M. Pullen was formed, the CPA license did not exist and the industry was unregulated. Virginia did not assign its first CPA licenses until 1910, when Wilson received license number 5 and Pullen, number 6. And within four years, the fledgling firm of Wilson & Pullen, Accountants had developed enough of a reputation for quality professional services to launch a successful branch office in Raleigh, North Carolina. In 1922 the firm changed its name to that of its original junior partner, A. M. Pullen, who had by then become a recognized leader in the profession of public accounting. The firm established administrative headquarters in Greensboro, North Carolina, in 1939, and continued to grow from that base, expanding up and down the Eastern seaboard.

By the 1970s, however, A.M. Pullen wasn't growing fast enough to keep pace with the rapidly expanding accounting and consulting industry. As a result, a merger became all but inevitable. The firm turned down merger overtures from two of the Big 8 firms, preferring to find a partner more compatible with its own mission and size, and one that wouldn't swallow its identity completely. It found that partner in McGladrey Hendrickson & Company.

A.M. Pullen in 1931

A.M. Pullen partner James J. Needham, partner-in-charge of the firm's New York office and a member of its executive committee, was the first CPA to serve on the Securities and Exchange Commission, from 1969 to 1973.

Chapter 2: Growth Spurts (1977-1999)

McGladrey Offers "Management Advice"

The development of the firm as a provider of consulting services (or "management advice," as it was first called) started in 1934 with George Hansen when he was transferred to the Davenport, Iowa, office. The Tri-Cities economy had been devastated by the Great Depression, and the Davenport practice was virtually out of clients: only twelve business clients were left, most of which were losing money, along with a handful of personal tax returns. In order to develop the one-man branch—and to increase fees—Hansen moved away from doing seasonal bookkeeping and basic accounting work, teaching clients' employees to do that work, and he replaced the number-crunching by offering management advice, which provided year-round work (and, Hansen admitted, he found this more interesting than basic accounting). Eventually, as the growth of the Davenport office proved the wisdom of Hansen's thinking, McGladrey began to offer management advice in the firm's other offices, although it was many years before it would begin to rival accounting and auditing as a percentage of the firm's business.

McGladrey's modern era of consulting began in 1966. "That was a point in time when firms were trying to get into consulting, and it was somewhat difficult to do because it was a different discipline than the audit and tax areas . . . but the leaders of the firm felt that, based on what was happening within the profession, it was necessary to get into it," recalled Larry Dowell, who had been working as a CPA for only four years when he was tapped to assist Bill Osmundson, a partner in the Quad Cities area, in getting the firm's consulting practice off the ground.

"At that point in time, Arthur Andersen was into consulting, and some of the other what would have been called the 'Big 8' firms were into it, but the other firms were just getting started," said Dowell, adding that it was in the best interest of the Big 8 that consulting

Bob Jensen concluded the 1985 consulting conference with some final thoughts. "Winning is a matter of planning, execution, teamwork, and individual commitment," he said. "We need to focus our efforts to make the best of our opportunities. We can't just be satisfied with our own individual success. We have to challenge this firm to success."

services become more accepted within the profession. Several of these firms (McGladrey's larger competitors) even offered their assistance to smaller, regional firms like McGladrey. "Arthur Andersen was very, very helpful in terms of providing counseling, training, and support."

Information technology auditing (then known as electronic data process auditing) was the firm's entry into this new arena. "Computers were just coming into being in terms of being real commercial," said Dowell, who attended an intensive training program with the Measurement Research Center in Iowa City in order to learn about early programming systems. "In the early days we concentrated fairly heavily in computers, systems consulting, and EDP auditing . . . Then as the consulting area progressed, we started expanding into other areas and doing more strategy types of consulting and operational consulting, manufacturing consulting, human-resources consulting—and, of course, we always did quite a bit of financial-management consulting. So over a period of time we developed into really a fairly full-blown management-consulting operation with quite a bit of diversity," Dowell said. "I think one of the reasons we added that diversity was that our clients were primarily the small to mid-size businesses, versus the giant clients, and they needed to use a fairly wide variety of services.

"We gradually grew over the years and when I retired in 1999, I believe we had about 650 people classified as management consultants and the consulting revenue was around $80 million."

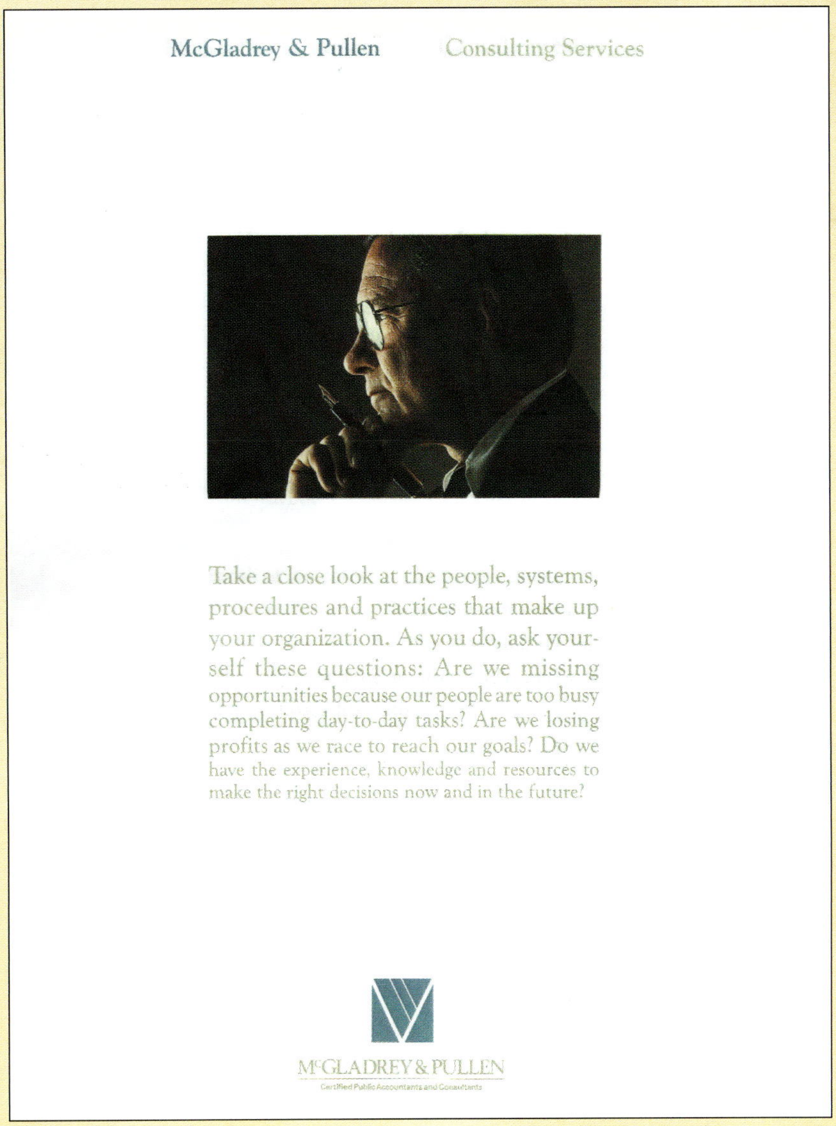

Advertising McGladrey's consulting services: Take a close look at the people, systems, procedures and practices that make up your organization. As you do, ask yourself these questions: Are we missing opportunities because our people are too busy completing day-to-day tasks? Are we losing profits as we race to reach our goals? Do we have the experience, knowledge and resources to make the right decisions now and in the future?

Chapter 2: Growth Spurts (1977-1999)

> *"We had big fights over things like the size of paper,"* recalled Leroy Martin. *"In accounting, what you do is fill up white sheets of paper with numbers, and then you keep them as evidence that you actually looked at the numbers. We used long paper, and McGladrey had short paper—fourteen-inch versus eleven-inch—so we fought,"* he chuckled. In the end, *"we traded the size of the paper for the way we coded the work papers. You couldn't go the other way because the filing cabinets were all smaller at McGladrey!"*

Sometimes it was the little things that seemed to matter most. After the Broeker Hendrickson merger, a five-person committee with members from both firms attempted to steer the newly combined organization through the transition. "We had big fights over things like the size of paper," recalled Martin. "In accounting, what you do is fill up white sheets of paper with numbers, and then you keep them as evidence that you actually looked at the numbers. We used long paper, and McGladrey had short paper—fourteen-inch versus eleven-inch—so we fought," he chuckled. In the end, "we traded the size of the paper for the way we coded the work papers. You couldn't go the other way because the filing cabinets were all smaller at McGladrey!"

Pullen's management included many older partners, so retirements were common. As a result, many McGladrey Hendrickson employees and partners from the Midwest were transferred to the Southeast as replacements, which helped to instill a single culture throughout the firm. "One of the interesting aspects of our firm, since we were Iowa-based, is that when you start looking out across the firm, you start seeing all these Midwestern roots," said Siders. "I'm from there, and we have partners located all across the U.S. who started their career in an office in Iowa or another Midwestern state. When we did mergers, we would transfer in someone to the new practice from the 'mother ship', a Midwestern office, to help integrate, or "McGladrey-ize" them. We were able to replace the transferred personnel, because our strong brand there allowed us to recruit and develop top talent from the Midwestern universities. When I was leading our campus recruiting at the University of Iowa in the eighties, I recall we were the second largest employer on that campus."

For a good five years after acquiring A.M. Pullen, McGladrey transferred dozens of people to fill spots in the Carolinas and other former Pullen offices. This in turn created a talent drain for its existing offices in the Midwest. The firm wanted to continue growing, but lacked both the manpower and funding for additional mergers, especially ones on a large scale. "We transferred a lot of people into new offices, so we didn't have a lot of human capital to use," said Jack Wahlig, who succeeded longtime leader Ivan Bull as managing partner in 1982. "We said, 'There are a lot of firms out there that would probably be good merger candidates, but we're kind of tapped out right now.'" In order to expand its reach without such an intense commitment of human resources, the company established the McGladrey Network, a group of independent firms affiliated with McGladrey for the purpose of gaining access to resources such as education, international expertise, and specialty advice. Network members pay a fraction of the cost required to develop comparable resources on their own, and while client demands were requiring they increase their capabilities, the network allowed them to do this while maintaining their independence.

During the 1980s, as regulation, standards, and laws became more complicated, increased specialization took place within both the profession and the firm. It was a time when the world was changing, said Mark Scally, and circumstances were requiring more imaginative products and services from the profession of public accounting. Wahlig, who "never met an idea he didn't like," said Doug Opheim, was the right man to be leading the firm. When Wahlig became managing partner in 1982, the firm had been growing steadily for more than fifty years. "It was a mature, stable firm," said Wahlig, "and the natural tendency was to say, 'If it ain't broke, don't fix it.' But we could sense that our marketplace and our business environment were changing. So we made a concerted effort to look into the future—to identify the type of firm our clients would like to be served by and the type of firm that would meet our people's needs.

"As someone said once, we probably over-excelled at growth, and at the same time we were trying to change the culture of the firm a little bit to be more proactive," Wahlig said. "It was a time when the competitive environment changed a lot. It's now totally permissible to solicit business, when back in the

> "We have one and only one ambition.
>
> To be the best satisfier of client needs.
>
> What else is there."

What McGladrey leaders were saying in the 1980s still holds true today: clients are the number-one priority.

Chapter 2: Growth Spurts (1977-1999)

early years it had not been. It was 'unprofessional,' or at least it was viewed that way. By the 1980s it was marketing, selling, cross-selling—all those words didn't exist and we didn't use them, but the partners who were successful business developers in the firm all knew how to get new business with just a little more indirect approach. But that was a big change, so we were trying to change the culture of the firm and become more proactive, and at the same time we were doing a lot of merger growth."

The most important thing to keep in mind, Wahlig stressed, was that "the firm is committed to helping our clients succeed. If we don't do that, we can do the greatest audits in the world, we can do the greatest tax work in the world, greatest consulting perhaps in the world, but if we don't help them be a better organization because they've retained us, then we've failed. What I used to preach to the guys is that our success is not the objective we strive for, our client's success is what we strive for and if we

New managers in 1982: Joe Adams, Schaumburg; Al Johnson and Mike Spoden, both of Rockford; Dave Valcik, Champaign; Hugh Frisbie, Schaumburg; and Roger Rhodes, Champaign

New offices in Pasadena suit Midwesterners just fine: Sitting in the courtyard of their new office building during the summer of 1988 are, from right, Kurt Korneisel, Greg Jones, Kent Harms, and Craig Steinman. All four worked in the Davenport office before transferring to Pasadena.

Discussion leader Mark Scally of Schaumburg (standing) and his group listen to Des Moines' Mitch Morlan explain uses of the Client Needs Assessment program during "breakout" sessions on Day 2 of the partners' meeting in June 1983. Other group members visible are (left to right) Kirby Marks of Des Moines, Dave Murphy of Janesville, Bob Brunson of Champaign, and Cal Rolloff of Moline.

accomplish that then we will be successful. And so many business organizations are focused on their own success. So I think if we can convey that, because that has been true—it was true before I got there and it was true when I left and I assume it's still true today."

In 1989 LeRoy E. Martin became the new managing partner, while Wahlig took the role of chairman. Martin, who joined McGladrey in the merger with Broeker Hendrickson, was the firm's first non-homegrown managing partner. Prior to the promotion, Martin had served as a regional managing partner, responsible for the McGladrey offices in Minnesota, South Dakota, and western Wisconsin. He took the reins at a time when both the marketplace and the field of public accounting were experiencing great instability, said Tom Siders. "At the time, I was the firm's national coordinator for the Savings & Loan industry. There was considerable uncertainty in the economy and our profession. The financial markets were jumpy, and regulators were regularly initiating litigation against audit firms;

New faces joining us in 1983 with Holdeman, Chiddister & Co. include (standing, left to right) Steve Fulton, partner; John Gardner, manager; John Holdeman, partner; and John Wolf, partner. (Seated, left to right) managers Dave Glesenkamp and John Fetter and partners Bob Gordon and Tim Frick

In November 1985 Rocky Mount Partners shows off its new sign in front of its new location on Thomas Street and thought this was also a good occasion to introduce recently merged partners from Harrison and Judge. In addition to Carlton Taylor (far left), they are (second from left) Glen Kennedy, Billy Gupton, Steve Daniel, Don Harrison, and Willis Hardesty.

One of the wonderful traditions of McGladrey is the softball tournament held once a year. After successful mergers, the number of teams got bigger.

Chapter 2: Growth Spurts (1977-1999)

A.Y. McDonald Mfg. Co. Grows with McGladrey

In a relationship that has spanned more than 30 years, A.Y. McDonald Mfg. Co. has counted on the business advice of McGladrey & Pullen partners like Roy Duff, Ed Ulve, Jim Kennedy, and Kerry Azbell. A leading manufacturer of waterworks brass, plumbing valves, pumps and water systems and high pressure gas valves and meter bars, the Dubuque-based firm has experienced a lot of changes in those thirty years.

"We have relied on our McGladrey partner's tax and management advice on a variety of issues," said Roy Sherman, a former McGladrey & Pullen employee who served as controller then chief financial officer at A.Y. McDonald from 1978 to 1995, in addition to vice president–finance, president, and chief executive officer. "Our McGladrey partners have been very astute in recognizing issues that a private company faces."

Sherman, who continues to work with A.Y. McDonald Mfg. Co., including serving on the company's board, emphasizes the importance of the relationships in a family corporation. "We have always asked for professional opinions from our partners, who have also provided business advice to individuals in the family."

Over the years, the manufacturer experienced rapid growth and many business changes that required McGladrey & Pullen partners to weigh in—issues from financing and relocation of their facility to property sales, acquisitions, and the sale of the A.Y. McDonald Supply division in 1993.

One of the reasons A.Y. McDonald Mfg. Co. switched to McGladrey & Pullen in the 1970s was the family's desire to use a local firm that could be more responsive. The company had been using a Big Four accounting firm located in Chicago. "Though A.Y. McDonald Mfg. Co. was privately held, we always maintained that we wanted our financial accounting to be the same as if we were public—no tricks, just straightforward accounting," Sherman added. "We wanted to be responsible to stockholders as if we were a public company. That was our direction and McGladrey met that need. Family members have always had a good relationship with McGladrey and, to this day, continue to be impressed with Kerry [Azbell] and staff."

professional liability insurance was costly if it was available at all. We needed a leader who could provide a calming effect and get us back to basics. LeRoy was the right person at that time."

Whereas Wahlig had been a dynamic leader, a true salesman, Martin's personality made him a calming influence on the firm. He wasn't looking to change the world, just to have a positive impact on the firm. "My goal was to take a lot of what was already out there and fix it, settle the firm down," he recalled. "I wanted to bring some steadiness and stability to the firm, something that was needed at the time. I told people, 'Here are the things we are going to do, and here are the things we are not going to do, and that's the way it's going to be.' So we worked on the AAV system, polished it up and made sure it would work, look for ways to fund it—because it was always an unfunded liability of the partnership. I also spent a lot of time on legal liability issues, which were getting worse, not better.

Management took a bit of a beating at the hands of new partners in the fall of 1992. Above, Jim Kolveit, Mark Jones, Jim Blayney, and LeRoy Martin enjoyed the antics anyway.

"The other thing I preached on a regular basis was that I wanted to make our environment more people-friendly. We needed to reduce employee turnover and increase job satisfaction. I've always believed that if you have good people, everything else follows."

Martin planned to keep McGladrey on a course of expansion by merging with firms that served its traditional client: closely held small to medium-sized businesses. While its core business was still tax and auditing, the company began to emphasize its consulting services, which made up about 15 percent of its business. By offering advice about human resources, marketing, and information systems to firms too small to do it themselves, he said, McGladrey & Pullen would be better able to serve its client niche.

Growing through merger allowed McGladrey to take large steps relatively quickly, to get into particular markets or services lines in a short amount of time rather than the longer process of building something. "When I took over as managing partner, I did a look back on our mergers. Over the prior ten years, we did 100 mergers—and a lot of them were add-ons," said Martin. "We got smarter as we went. Back then you could

Chapter 2: Growth Spurts (1977-1999)

The McGladrey Network

The McGladrey Network was the brainchild of former managing partner Jack Wahlig, who, recognizing that in the late 1980s the firm did not have the resources to grow only through merger, realized there were other ways to expand its coverage throughout the United States. Led by Henry Allovio Jr., a partner in the Peoria, Illinois, practice, the firm established a system in which network member firms maintain their names and autonomy and are responsible for their own client-fee arrangements, delivery of services, and maintenance of client relationships, with access to the infrastructure of a national firm.

"I knew we were serious about it when the firm said they were willing to let Henry Allovio devote his time to trying to get this off the ground," said Wahlig. "Henry was a highly compensated partner, and so this was a commitment. And Henry did an absolutely excellent job. In the beginning, it was very important to get people in the firm to be willing to serve the network, sometimes on short notice, instead of something they could have done with their own local clients. Henry had enough clout to be successful at that."

Allovio went out to other independent firms and sold them the concept, Wahlig said. For a license fee, these firms gained access to McGladrey's practice aids and manuals as well as its specialists. "A lot of those guys saw this as the best of all worlds," Wahlig said. "They were still 'Finn Flint & Finbar' in their local community—they hadn't sold out or merged—but now they could tell their clients, 'We have the resources of this large firm that focuses on entrepreneurial clients like you, and we have those resources so we can serve you better.' The idea caught on, and over time a couple of other partners were involved. We treated the network just like it was a client. If you were a network firm, you were a client, and our responsibility was to help you succeed."

By 1989 the network was up and running with its initial handful of firms. When Dan Brooks, executive director from 1997 to 2006, joined Henry Allovio and Jim Clarahan on the network team in 1991, the number of firms was more than ten. "It was still a fledgling business unit—it was pretty much a start-up—but we were starting to see some trends and some market acceptability, so we brought in more resources," he said. During the period from 1992 to 1997, the network experienced explosive growth thanks to the addition of Dick Adams as a dedicated director of business development.

While accounting associations have been around for a long time (and McGladrey was part of some of those associations in the early days), this was the first of its kind. Network members pay a license fee to essentially "rent the infrastructure of a national firm for a fraction of what it would cost you to develop the resources yourself," said Brooks. That includes client service tools, human resource systems, marketing systems. "They can get a lot of these things from a lot of different sources in the profession; what we offer is a one-stop shop. We also have high client service standards and a vested interest in really making sure we deliver good quality, and if something goes wrong,

The Network Firms help expand our reach. (newspaper headline announcing launch of network)

Henry Allovio passed command of the McGladrey Network to Jim Fitzpatrick on May 1, 1995.

we fix it." When talking with prospective new members, Brooks uses the analogy of "a really nice buffet line." "McGladrey lays everything out there for you, and you get to pick and choose what you want."

Firms join the network for a variety of reasons. "Some join because they want to get really good training and like our client service tools, and the training ties into those tools. Some join for offensive reasons, to grow and go after bigger clients. Some join for defensive reasons, to be able to maintain and present a larger presence to their bigger clients who are targets for larger firms," said Brooks. Regardless of the reason, the network gives its members "the best of both worlds," he said. "They can say to their larger clients, 'We may be a local firm, but we have the backing of the largest middle-market firm in the world . . . You are going to get the same client service that you would expect from local professionals, but at the same time we can tap into this wealth of talent and knowledge that our local competitors can't touch.'"

Deb Lockwood, current executive director, commented that as the network's membership and internal team resources grew, so did its value to the members and McGladrey. The network firms share best practices, partner in client service opportunities, and contribute industry knowledge, trends, and niche expertise to McGladrey. The firms access the network client service team for practice management consulting such as strategic planning, partner compensation system design, mergers and acquisitions assistance, and leadership training.

Employees of RSM McGladrey Network 1998

The network has also been beneficial to McGladrey's expansion activities, said LeRoy Martin. "The network gave us some real credibility in the profession." It also made McGladrey "the godfather of a whole bunch of firms, and it gave us the ability to sort out and identify good potential merger candidates. Network firms have been "our best acquisition candidates," said Brooks, adding, "It's kind of like dating before you get married."

The network mission is to help build and sustain high performing CPA and consulting firms as measured by financial performance, people development, and service quality using the combined resources of the network, RSM McGladrey, and McGladrey & Pullen. Dan Brooks acknowledged that, "with a lot of support from a lot of other people and the members, we built it up to being the premier accounting association of its type in the world." Today the McGladrey Network comprises just under 100 firms and provides tools and resources to many more. Not only has the network program been a very good investment for the firm, it also increases McGladrey's profile within the profession. "Of the top 300 or 400 firms in the entire profession, we have some relationship with over 200. Between McGladrey and the network, we now have coverage in every state in the United States."

> *While its clients were not Fortune 500 companies, the firm's attitude was that it would love to see any of its clients "grow up" to become part of the Fortune 500 someday.*

go ahead and mess up a merger, and it didn't cost you a lot. You got some clients out of it, people went away, and you had the territory. But we got smarter about that. We started doing mergers where we already were located, so we had the leadership in place locally." McGladrey would start a small practice in an area and then merge it into a bigger local office.

The combining of cultures is always a challenge," said Mike Kirley, chief enterprise services officer. "It's always a very stressful time even under the best of circumstances, and it's disruptive to people. Our goal, of course, has always been to make sure that it's not disruptive to the clients."

STAYING TRUE TO ITS ROOTS

By the early 1990s, McGladrey & Pullen had offices in the "glamour locations" like New York and Chicago, but the overwhelming majority of its seventy-plus offices were still in the smaller cities where most of America's smaller, privately held entrepreneurial companies were doing business, like San Bernardino and Pasadena, California; Asheville, North Carolina; Sioux Falls, South Dakota; Moline, Illinois; Gillette, Wyoming; and Stillwater, Minnesota. McGladrey had

When Grant Thornton merged with our Las Vegas office, only a change in signs by Phil Pechman, left, Las Vegas partner, and Richard Delaney, regional managing partner of Grant Thornton, was needed to complete the transition.

consistently churned out moderate growth, year in and year out—but also steadily penetrated deeper into its Heartland base and gently expanded its reach through its network program. It had proved itself to be a survivor. At a time when the large multinational CPA firms (then down to the Big 6) pursued high-profile public companies while fending off malpractice lawsuits, McGladrey & Pullen sought to proactively position itself as a premier provider of a full range of tax, accounting, and consulting services for the closely held businesses—a niche in which it had long been successful, as the numbers attested: In 1992 up to 85 percent of McGladrey's revenue came from closely held businesses grossing from $3 million to $70 million. The firm had fewer than 200 public companies on its client roster but handled tax returns for 36,000 individuals. While its clients were not Fortune 500 companies, the firm's attitude was that it would love to see any of its clients "grow up" to become part of the Fortune 500 someday.

As an industry, all CPA firms were becoming more specialized. As it approached the end of the decade and the start of a new century, one of the firm's key business strategies was to focus on increasing its expertise in key industry and functional areas. To help it do so, it began to create

Steve Sorensen, Roger Montgomery, and Jerry Harbaugh enjoy the festive atmosphere after the partners' meeting in the fall of 1991.

more of a national infrastructure: After more than two years of discussion and soul-searching, the branch-office system was revamped by imposing a single partner-in-charge over four formerly equal partners, each responsible for marketing, operations, finance, or human resources. Most client needs were still handled by its local offices, but McGladrey also developed national resources, placing in key specialty areas people who were available to assist local offices and clients as needed. Industry specialty areas included manufacturing, wholesale distribution, and financial institutions. Functional

Chapter 2: Growth Spurts (1977-1999)

Sales and Marketing

Contractors and CPA firms took notice of our San Diego office thanks to our inventive direct-mail campaign, which utilized 750 10-inch long spent shotgun shells wrapped in the ad. The campaign aimed to inform contractors of new tax law changes and how we could help.

For many years, sales and marketing in the accounting profession were severely limited: In 1922 the AICPA had banned its members from advertising, saying it wasn't dignified. The group also forbade accountants to poach each other's clients. That meant when the organization relaxed its ban in the late 1970s, the industry had some ground to make up. Despite a 1978 Supreme Court decision giving the accounting profession the go-ahead to plug its services, accountants historically have been reluctant to advertise, preferring to sponsor seminars and mail letters or brochures, and for many years a feeling that "marketing is crass" lingered with many in the field. Almost twenty years after CPAs were given the right to advertise and actively market their services, McGladrey & Pullen created its first office of national marketing, led by Larry Bildstein and based in Cedar Rapids, Iowa. Since its establishment in 1997, the office of national marketing has sought to establish a stronger, more consistent firm-wide image, and the maturity and professionalism of McGladrey's marketing efforts "have grown leaps and bounds from where I first started," said Connie Smith Benning, the marketing director for the Central Plains Economic Unit; she previously was the firm's director of corporate communication and part of the firm's first office of national marketing.

Introducing a series of descriptors for use with the RSM McGladrey logo was one piece of the firm's ongoing branding effort in 1999.

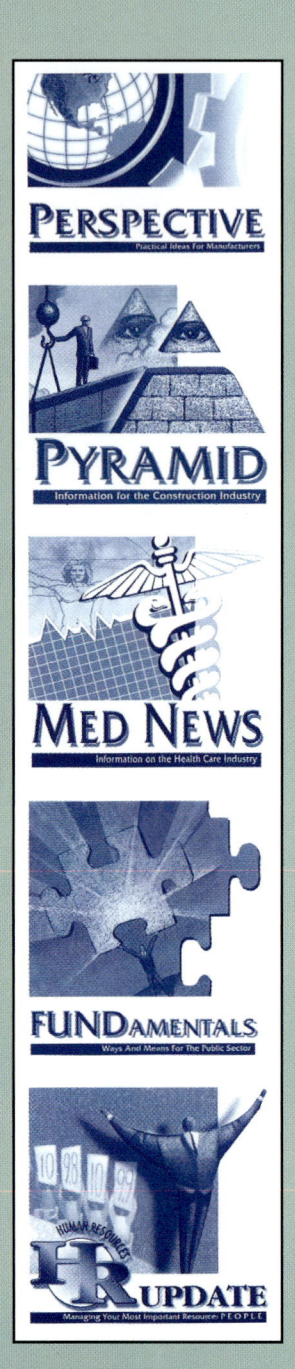

A redesign transforms firm newsletters into stronger marketing tools.

McGladrey: Beyond the Balance Sheet, 1926-2008

Rod LeMond, standing, leads a client situation review for Roger's Bindery, Inc., a San Bernardino client. Participating in the discussion are, from left, Bob Forest, CFO; Roger Imbriani, president; and Bill Heitritter and Larry Koenig of our San Bernardino office.

specialty areas included tax, audit, and consulting services, which included human resources and information technology. In 1994 the information technology consulting group included five people; two years later the firm had sixty information technology people serving client needs. The firm created new product lines, like a human-resources product line that included everything from benefits cost-control to outplacement services.

Even with increasing specialization and sub-specialization, McGladrey believed, the key to success remained close client relationships. By building a relationship with a client, McGladrey professionals become part of the client's management team, offering creative solutions to business problems and opportunities. A low staff-to-partner ratio—one of the lowest in the country—translated into greater partner involvement with clients, and the reorganization of its practices into larger "economic units" covering broader geography further cemented McGladrey's commitment to client contact. "Our people who are closest to the market are best able to identify the current needs of the market for our clients and anticipate future need," said Kirley. "Keeping things within those economic units lets the firm hold on to some of its more regional roots, have more personal relationships with clients. There's really no substitute for that face-to-face contact."

"Keeping things within those economic units lets the firm hold on to some of its more regional roots, have more personal relationships with clients. There's really no substitute for that face-to-face contact," said Mike Kirley.

Chapter 2: Growth Spurts (1977-1999)

Technology Blossoms

Changes in technology have had a tremendous impact on how business is done at McGladrey. From the two broken-down comptometers that Ira McGladrey deemed sufficient equipment in the 1930s ("Mr. McGladrey felt that anyone claiming to be an 'expert' accountant should surely be able to add and subtract," George Hansen wrote) to ten-key adding machines ("The first day I was in Davenport, they put me in a staff room and gave me a telephone book and a ten-key adding machine and said, 'You have to learn how to run that, so add up the telephone numbers in the book,'" recalled Jack Wahlig) to the company's first fax machine and the arrival of the computer on the corporate scene in the late 1950s, technological advances have reduced the man-hours to perform many common accounting tasks and freed personnel up to deliver more complex services and advice.

Bill Boldt working on one of the firm's comptometers

Changes in technology really began to have an impact starting in the early 1980s. McGladrey began using calculators with an electronic display rather than just an adding-machine tape in 1980. The first microcomputer—an Apple computer—appeared around 1982, but attempts to make this successful in the field were limited because of its size. The first microcomputer used extensively emerged a year later. This machine, a Compaq computer featuring a six-inch green screen and a five-and-a-half-inch floppy disk that could hold 520 kilobytes of information, was assigned to the in-charges and had to be checked out to use in the field.

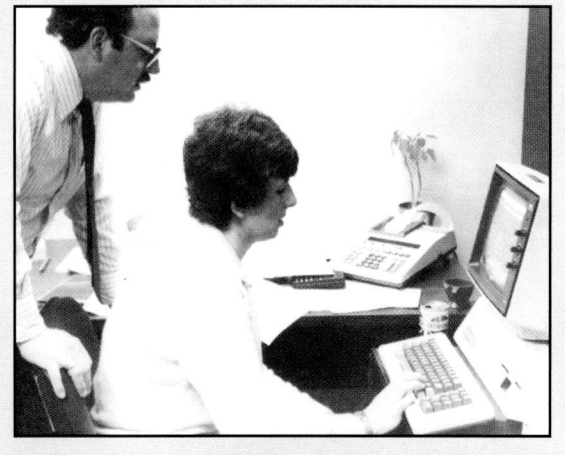

"Prior to spreadsheets, work was done on either 4 or 13-column workpapers," said Doug Opheim, chief U.S. operations officer. "Everything was done in pencil, and as you might imagine, some workpapers had numerous revisions and erase marks. Imagine the excitement when Visicalc arrived, which had 26 columns and 256 rows. In addition, when you changed one cell it would change the cells that were referenced to that: it changed how CPAs did their work."

The first trial balancing package was FAST/CPA, an internally developed software package. This proved to be a real success, and McGladrey went into the software business and sold this package to many CPA firms. This package was eventually sold in the mid-1990s for several million dollars and was the foundation of the GO Audit system.

The firm's first microcomputer appeared in the early 1980s.

In the early 1980s, tax processing was still done manually, with the forms filled out by hand or by typewriter. The first transition to technology was through a service center. Originally, a tax preparer completed input forms, which were mailed to the service center, and then a completed return was mailed back to the office.

"Invariably, here's what would happen," said Kimpa Moss, who started working for the firm in tax in the Champaign, Illinois, office in 1986. "You filled out those input forms and sent them off, they

McGladrey: Beyond the Balance Sheet, 1926-2008

generated a tax form, and two days later it came back to you. You'd take one look at the tax return and realize you hadn't checked a box, and the whole thing was wrong. So you'd have to start over again: resend the forms—now with that box checked!—wait two more days, and then it would come back with the changed number.

"I remember one time, it was April 15 in the morning—so the tax deadline day—and a couple of us were standing around talking when a partner came around the corner. It was obvious he had been in the office all night long. He's not shaven, he's wearing yesterday's clothes. He was holding a pile of papers in his hands and said, 'Okay, I got these input sheets; now where do I take them to get them processed?' 'Well, the last run was last night at 6:00 p.m. for you to get those in and actually get a tax return generated.' So he had to do an extension—obviously, to his chagrin. He thought he was going to get that return done, and instead he had to extend it." Eventually the forms were inputted at the local office, which saved several days in the process, and then shipped back to the office. By the end of the decade, a local office tax-processing system had appeared.

For its internal systems, McGladrey had a mainframe computer in Davenport, Iowa. The original systems required punch cards to execute programs, and all data was read into the machines via punch cards. Timesheets were mailed to Central Accounting each period and then keypunched onto eighty-column cards to be read into the mainframe. When the firm migrated off this system to Apple computers, each office would input its bills, create invoices, and track accounts receivable and transmit the information to Davenport to be consolidated with the rest of the firm's information.

The 1990s continued many of the technological advances developed in the previous decade, with faster, more powerful computers, which now included color screens, used for spreadsheets, word processing, trial balancing, and tax preparation. The critical change was a Vision 2000 Technology plan, developed in the mid-1990s, that required significant investments. Among the plan's key components, the firm decided to purchase PeopleSoft for its payroll and benefits system as well as for general ledger, accounts payable, and fixed assets. At the time, McGladrey was the smallest company using PeopleSoft, but the system proved scaleable for future acquisitions.

The firm also developed the Integrated Practice Management system—leading-edge software for keeping track of time and billing. Remote Time & Expense (RTE) was written as a vehicle to allow McGladrey's client servers to enter their time remotely while serving clients; the first RTE system sent the time and expense transactions via Lotus Notes e-mail. The move to Lotus Notes gave the firm the capability to store data both centrally and remotely in Notes databases that would sync back up when connected—a huge advantage for auditors and consultants as they could work remotely on laptops and then sync the information back to the centralized database when they returned to the office.

Personal Computers: Making Your Life Better

By BOB JENSEN
MAS Coordinator

Are you dabbling in personal computers; Are you getting your feet wet; or, Are you hiding, hoping that the personal computer won't find you? Don't be afraid! Get out of the closet! Get out of the Dark Ages! Challenge yourself. Look at the kids...look how they are challenging themselves. The children are having fun and so can you.

There is no doubt that using the personal computer within our Firm has opened both old and young eyes. Creating new and exciting ways to use the personal computer in auditing, taxes, and planning services will help us increase our involvement with clients. This is one of the exciting parts of McGladrey Hendrickson & Co. at the moment and in the future.

The personal computer and what it can bring us should be looked at.

Let's Review

As a tax person, you know that it was very difficult to run through all those calculations needed to give a client more than just one alternative. With the micro-computer, this is not so. Using the Ardvark Income and Estate Planning Programs, you can simultaneously prepare many different computations, inserting many variables and can review them with the client present. This makes us very responsive!

Tax specialists are **now** busy creating new programs that will couple the individual income tax package, the estate package and an individual financial planning model into complete planning services for the individual. This is real "one-stop shopping" concept like that prevalent in today's business focus.

Auditors

You've heard about the robot taking over those repetitive manufacturing tasks. Likewise, the personal computer will someday contain most of our audit workpapers in its memory. Already this is evidenced by the auditing use in analytical review, report and tax grouping preparation, income tax computations, etc.

Again, our audit specialists are working hard to develop concepts using data base managers (a buzz word you should get to know) to help us be more efficient in confirmation analysis, report preparation, lead sheets and working trial balance tasks.

Oh, and let's not forget our clients.

If you could only get our clients in to see how easy these systems are to use, we could double or triple the business we are doing in financial planning and projection work. The personal computer is extremely approachable. It beckons the reluctant client to sit down and try it. More often than not they become hooked - especially if we can give them ON THE SPOT a couple of real good specific uses. From then on, we naturally get involved in almost all the computer decisions that are made.

We've made no distinction between word processing computers and personal computers because conceptually, there really is no difference. You need to know the same computer concepts to run a data processing system, a word processing system or a personal computer. It's a little scary, but it looks like we are all headed for doing some EDP consulting - WOW!

What's on your horizon? Let's get with the program. We are now doing some neat things, and it looks like we are going to be continually doing some neat things. Graphics prepared on the computer with the financial projections combine to make nifty presentation material for new financial packages on potential deals. Consolidation routines can couple more than one company's projections together. Survey results can be completed and analyzed.

I know you're fond of your ten-keys and thirteen column, but once you've tasted this new technology, there's no going back!

"Don't be afraid!" "Get out of the Dark Ages!" Bob Jensen, MAS coordinator, urged McGladrey personnel to find out how personal computers could improve their work lives in 1982.

Partners in Education

The firm's commitment to Iowa has a long history, beginning in 1926 with its founder, Ira B. McGladrey. Today, McGladrey & Pullen is helping Iowa business by partnering with the state's colleges and universities to develop beneficial business education programs. One such effort is the I. B. McGladrey Institute, founded in 1980 to enhance the University of Iowa Department of Accounting's research and educational programs. The institute adopted I. B. McGladrey as part of its name in 1984 to recognize the substantial contributions of McGladrey & Pullen alumni to sustaining the institute's endowment base. Today the institution is a distinctive feature of the Iowa accounting program, fostering instructional development, curriculum enhancement, and faculty research by providing financial support to faculty and their graduate assistants.

McGladrey & Pullen also works with the institute to sponsor educational conferences for Iowa businesses. The first one was held in October 1996 and was titled "Customer Satisfaction: Mandates for Manufacturing—Implementing Strategy for Profit." The conference featured nationally recognized leaders in manufacturing from industry and academics, and focused on how to achieve customer-focused quality management. The firm also partners with Iowa State University and the Iowa Small Business Development Center to sponsor another conference, "Shaping the Future," which teaches strategic planning skills to chief executive officers of small and medium-sized businesses. It is designed to help Iowa companies gain a competitive advantage in an increasingly competitive global economy. The Iowa Family Business Forum, co-sponsored by McGladrey & Pullen, gives managers of family-owned enterprises an opportunity to learn and discuss solutions to the special organizations and communications that are inherent in family businesses.

A similar partnership has been forged with the University of Northern Iowa. The McGladrey & Pullen Center for Accounting Education was funded through contributions by McGladrey and UNI alumni. The center's goal is to encourage and help the UNI Department of Accounting maintain and strengthen its efforts to provide excellence in accounting education. In addition, the company has recently funded the school's McGladrey & Pullen Professorship in Accounting.

Chapter Three

A Bold Leap Forward

(1999-Present)

As McGladrey faced the start of a new century, the board of directors decided it was time for the firm to head in a new direction. "We were not growing, and we were not very profitable, " said Doug Opheim, McGladrey's chief operations officer. "The organization needed a new energy, a new direction."

Opheim was a new member of the board in 1997 when McGladrey took its first step in that new direction. Led by Duane M. Tyler, partner-in-charge of the firm's Chicago office, the board elected three individuals to the "office of the managing partner" rather than selecting a single individual to the office—a first in McGladrey history. The combination was designed to be highly effective, Opheim said. "You had Mark Scally, who was a visionary salesperson; Tom Rotherham, who was a financial leader; and Bob Jensen, who is a very operations-driven person."

Office of Managing Partner: Mark Scally, Bob Jensen, and Tom Rotherham

STRATEGIC ADVISORY GROUP

One of the first things the office of managing partner did was set up a strategic advisory group to evaluate the possible directions in which the firm could go. In addition to Scally, Rotherham, and Jensen, the committee included Tyler; Jim Blayney, partner-in-charge of the Quad Cities office; and Pat Tabor, partner-in-charge of the San Diego office. Opheim also became involved in the discussions to model the financial alternatives for the group.

The question they asked was, "What are we going to do with this firm?" "The objective was to see what kind of firm we ought to create," said Scally.

The group spent nearly two years studying the firm's current situation and weighing options for its future. It identified the fact that McGladrey & Pullen was only present in seven of the top twenty-five major metropolitan markets in the United States—"so we weren't even remotely a national firm," said Bill Travis, who became the firm's managing partner in 1999. "Other than the markets where we had a big presence, nobody knew who we were . . . At the time, the Big 4 had a lot more capabilities and resources than we had, and the smaller firms that were 'large locals' and some of the regionals were less expensive than we were. So we were at that stage in our life cycle where we had a major glass ceiling above us. We needed to have more geographic presence so that we could have a positive differentiation in the marketplace."

The group came up with eighteen strategic alternatives, including merging up to one of the Big 4 ("the larger firms were really only interested in some of our major metro offices," Travis said), breaking the firm apart into a couple of smaller, regional firms ("nobody truly liked that idea"), and becoming a public company. "We looked at raising money through debt or perhaps taking the consulting practice public and raising some capital that way, but it didn't really make sense," said Travis.

Strategic Advisory Group members Duane Tyler, Schaumburg; Pat Tabor, San Diego; Bob Jensen, Schaumburg; and Jim Blayney, Davenport, agree that the business combination with H&R Block offers our firm the resources to become the leading firm in the United States serving mid-sized companies.

"We should all take pride in the fact that we've altered the competitive landscape of the accounting and consulting industry." – Mark Scally

"We'd either have too much debt, or we wouldn't have enough money to do what we really needed to do."

Ultimately, the group concluded that McGladrey needed to become a truly national firm. "And for that, we needed capital," Opheim said.

Enter H&R Block. The leading tax preparation company in the United States, H&R Block had begun developing other financial products and services for its 16 million U.S. tax clients and since May 1998 had purchased eight accounting firms, which functioned under its "Business Services" label. Combining McGladrey and Block's accounting practices would significantly accelerate their shared strategy of building an industry-leading firm, with McGladrey serving as a solid foundation upon which to expand a national practice.

Block's strategy aligned well with McGladrey & Pullen's goals. "What we gave them was a platform," Opheim said. "We had client-service infrastructure, we had management, we had accounting-business processes and systems—we had all the infrastructure to do this. They provided us with the capital to become a national firm."

"McGladrey & Pullen and H&R Block are very similar," Scally wrote in an August 1999 special issue of the company's internal newsletter, *Mpressions*. "Both organizations have an incredibly high level of integrity and dedication to client service . . . [Block's leaders are] committed to making RSM McGladrey a major player in the middle market. They strongly support our efforts and realize that we are strategically important to H&R Block's overall success."

At the partners' meeting in February 1999, McGladrey & Pullen voted to sell all the business—except for its attest assets—to H&R Block for more than $400 million. The motion passed with 98 percent approval, and the transaction was completed in August 1999.

"This business combination is a first in our industry," Scally wrote. "Never before has a firm of our size partnered with a major financial services company that will be providing access to capital for expansion nationally and the ability to pursue an aggressive middle-market strategy. We should all take pride in the fact that we've altered the competitive landscape of the accounting and consulting industry."

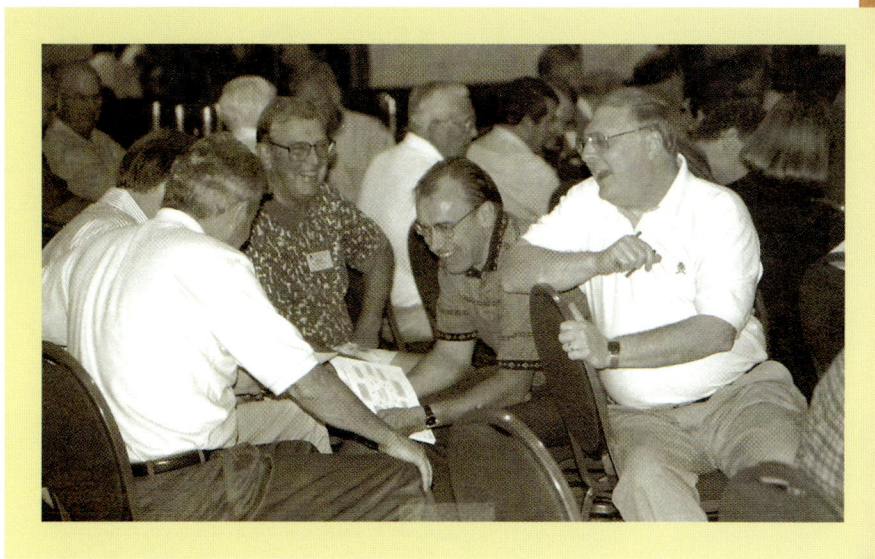

Partners take advantage of a break in a meeting to share thoughts, ideas, and a few laughs.

All economic units met in early March 1999 to learn more about McGladrey & Pullen's new strategic vision and discussions with H&R Block. Davenport partner and board member Steve Hammes answers a question from Firmwide Resources' Debbie Lensmeyer.

How I Spent the Summer of '99

By Mark Scally

As you can see on the cover of this issue of *Mpressions*, Tom Rotherham and I signed the business combination agreement between McGladrey & Pullen and H&R Block on June 29. That signing was the result of a lot of hard work by many people in the Firm, not just the Office of the Managing Partner. For their help, I would like to say thank you.

This business combination is a first in our industry. Never before has a firm of our size partnered with a major financial services company that will be providing access to capital for expansion nationally and the ability to pursue an aggressive middle-market strategy. We should all take pride in the fact that we've altered the competitive landscape of the accounting and consulting industry!

Someone recently asked me what I learned over the past few months of negotiations with H&R Block.

One of the things I discovered was that the signed agreement between HRB and M&P was more than just a business transaction between two organizations focused on building the leading provider of tax, consulting, and audit services to mid-sized businesses.

It represented a learning experience that was much more complicated than I originally anticipated. This was partly due to the large number of constituencies: employees, clients, partners, recruits, retired partners, and of course, the government. There were so many groups to keep in mind. Working with the Strategic Advisory Group and many other special groups within the Firm, Tom and I tried to address as many of the issues affecting these audiences as possible during our discussions with H&R Block.

Another thing I learned is that McGladrey & Pullen and H&R Block are very similar. Both organizations have an incredibly high level of integrity and dedication to client service. The more Tom and I worked with Frank Salizzoni, H&R Block's president and chief executive officer, and Mark Ernst, chief operating officer, the more we realized that this strategic move was the right one. Frank and Mark are committed to making RSM McGladrey a major player in the middle market. They strongly support our efforts and realize that we are strategically important to H&R Block's overall success.

Unfortunately, when people think of a business combination, some tend to be automatically apprehensive. It's only natural. However, I want to reemphasize that this business combination is a positive move for our employees and clients.

Employees will be happy to know that this business combination will not affect jobs or job responsibilities and — more importantly — will

> **Thoughts from Around the Firm**
>
> **Wade Pack, supervisor, Greensboro:** "I'm very excited about the Firm's strategic vision, mainly because it shows a highly proactive attitude, which is one of the key ingredients to success. Positioning ourselves in this way, I believe, will help ensure we will be the leading provider to mid-sized companies."

Mpressions—Special Issue: August 1999

"How I Spent the Summer of '99" by Mark Scally

NOT result in employee reduction. In fact, we'll have a greater need for more talented, qualified people. This presents an excellent opportunity for people to take advantage of the employee referral bonus program. If you aren't familiar with that program, check with your local human resources/office manager.

Additionally, our People Group, led by Kathy Kenny, is in the process of reviewing our benefits program to identify areas that can be improved. Kathy will be communicating more on that in the near future.

As for our clients, they will still receive the same high-quality level of service defined by our Unique Strategic Positioning statement. And with our plans to expand into new markets, we'll be faced with some exciting client service opportunities.

So what now?

Looking ahead, the first item on my agenda is to answer as many of your questions as possible. Communication is most valuable when it is meaningful and often. Unfortunately, due to the complexities of the negotiations with the Block organization, it has been a little difficult to share information with you as often as I would have liked. With the negotiation process completed, I'll be able to devote more time to keeping everyone updated via *Mpressions*, *OMP Online*, *Mpulse*, and other communication tools.

I'm currently working with Tom and the Firm Management Team to finalize the organizational structures and roles for the leaders of RSM McGladrey, Inc., which will provide consulting and tax services, and McGladrey & Pullen, LLP, which will provide audit and attest services. The senior vice president positions within RSM McGladrey have been finalized: Craig Damos, Economic Units; Bob Jensen, Mergers/Transition; Kathy Kenny, People; Mike Kirley, Client Service; and Doug Opheim, Finance. Additionally, after August 1, 1999, Executive Partner Bill Travis, who will continue to lead McGladrey & Pullen's National Office of Audit and Accounting, will also be the managing partner of McGladrey & Pullen, LLP. We'll share finalized organizational charts for both firms with you in upcoming issues of *OMP Online*.

Another change to the organizational chart is the addition of Terry Putney, who joins RSM McGladrey after leading HRB Business Services during its first year. Bob Jensen and Terry will oversee our efforts to phase in the existing HRB Business Services foundation firms. Some of these firms will join us in the very near future, while others may take a year or two to complete the merger process. Bob and Terry will also be interviewing other CPA and consulting firms that are interested in joining RSM McGladrey. The strategy is to identify firms in the top 25 U.S. markets and in markets where we can be the dominant player in the tax, accounting, and consulting industry.

Hopefully, this letter has helped answer some of your questions. If you have other questions, I encourage you to visit the Business Combination database on Notes or check with your partner-in-charge.

In short, I'd like to congratulate everyone on being a part of this historic change in our Firm. I'd also like to thank everyone for hanging in there during the lengthy period of uncertainty and providing so much constructive feedback. I'm excited about what's ahead for us all. I hope you are too.

Enjoy the rest of your summer! **M**

Thoughts from Around the Firm

Heidi Hager, staff, Casper: "I commend the members of the planning committee and the partners for taking the initial steps to enable McGladrey to become the leading national CPA firm serving the middle market. I also commend the national office for keeping the staff informed as the process goes forward."

Mpressions—Special Issue: August 1999

Chapter 3: A Bold Leap Forward (1999–Present)

CREATION OF THE ALTERNATIVE PRACTICE STRUCTURE

McGladrey became a separate division of H&R Block. The firm's tax and consulting business was renamed RSM McGladrey Inc. and integrated with Block's previously acquired accounting firms. Together they formed a national accounting, tax, and consulting practice that shared a single client-service philosophy and had approximately 470 managing directors and nearly 4,000 employees in more than seventy offices nationwide. As the name indicated, RSM McGladrey continued to be a prominent member of RSM International.

McGladrey & Pullen's attest business, including audits, reviews, and other engagements in which the firm issues written opinions evaluating client financial statements, remained in a partnership owned by the McGladrey & Pullen partners.

Making it official, becoming RSM McGladrey and a part of H&R Block: Mark Scally, Frank Salizzoni, Mark Ernst and Tom Rotherham

McGladrey & Pullen and RSM McGladrey operate in an alternative practice structure in which the two separate legal entities work together to serve clients' business needs. Bill Travis became the new managing partner of McGladrey & Pullen, while the office of managing partners became RSM McGladrey officers: Mark Scally, chief executive officer; Tom Rotherham, chief operating officer; and Bob Jensen, senior vice president, Mergers/Transition.

The alternative practice structure arrangement was the result of careful study. "When we started contemplating the transaction with H&R Block, we went directly to the SEC to talk about the transaction and informed them about it. We wanted to get their point of view on what we needed to do to ensure that we could continue to serve publicly traded companies,"

Unique Strategic Positioning

Our goal is to be the best CPA/Consulting firm in the USA helping owner-managed, entrepreneurial clients succeed.

Our Clients: Owner-managed, entrepreneurial attitude, including those financed in the public markets.

- An experienced business advisor and confidant, a partner, will understand your business, and help you succeed.
- Our people prefer working with your size/type company.
- We understand your industry.
- We are a better value than our competitors.
- We have designed many high value-added financial information, tax, and consulting services specifically for you.
- We deliver high-quality and timely work for you.
- We consistently take it to you: ideas, questions, challenges, and solutions.
- You will work with very talented people.
- With your mission/goals in mind, our team works with you in an integrated way, without departmental barriers.

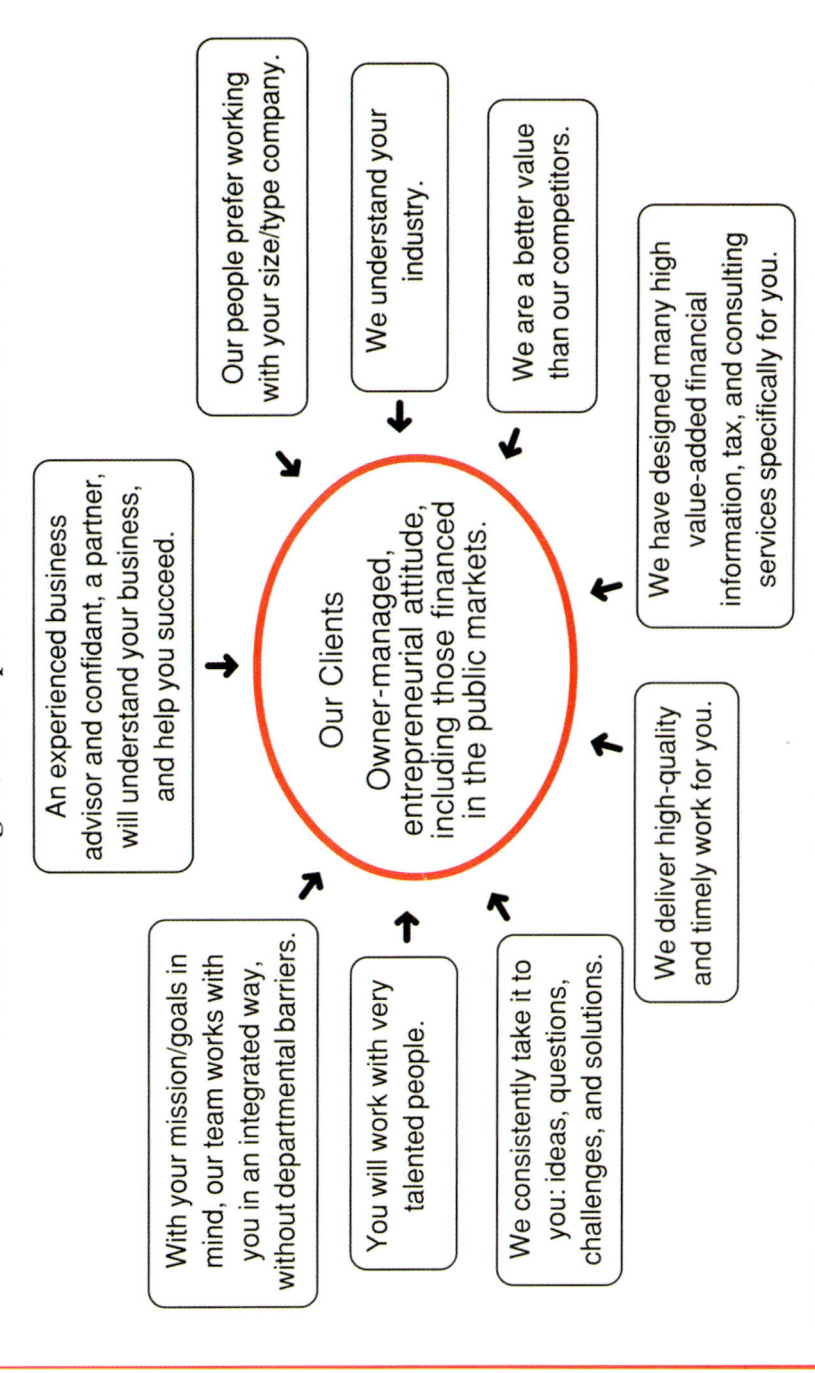

NOTE: The "uniqueness" of our positioning comes from successfully executing, in concert, each element of our USP for our clients' benefit. Our competitors may claim to focus on the elements included in our USP, but we actually do them.

McGladrey's Strategic Position in the Market, 1999

Chapter 3: A Bold Leap Forward (1999-Present)

said Travis. "We got their views on what would and wouldn't work structurally and in the end were able to make the modifications to the structure so that the SEC was very comfortable with what we were doing and why we were doing it."

To many, both inside and outside the firm, the news that McGladrey's tax and consulting business had been purchased by H&R Block was shocking. "Unfortunately, when people think of a business combination, some tend to be automatically apprehensive. It's only natural. However, I want to reemphasize that this business combination is a positive move for our employees and clients," wrote Scally. "Employees will be happy to know that this business combination will not affect jobs or job responsibilities and—more importantly—will not result in employee reduction. In fact, we'll have a greater need for more talented, qualified people. This presents an excellent opportunity for people to take advantage of the employee referral bonus program . . . As for our clients, they will still receive the same high-quality level of service defined by our Unique Strategic Positioning statement. And with our plans to expand into new markets, we'll be faced with some exciting client service opportunities."

Understanding that RSM McGladrey would operate in a different part of the marketplace than Block's tax practice soothed many fears, said human resources director Bob Wilson. "Roger Hendren and I went to make a presentation to a group of staff people about the H&R Block merger before the news came out. We were actually a couple of months ahead of the news, but we were aware that word might get to our employees and we wanted to go to them first and say, 'Here's what you're going to hear, this is the business case behind it, and we want you to be informed.' We had a PowerPoint presentation, which Roger, who is very good on his feet, delivered," Wilson said. "People were stunned by the news. 'We're going to be owned by H&R Block?' So at the end of the presentation, we asked for any questions. Of course, people are a little hesitant to ask questions, but finally one person raised his hand and said, 'Does this mean if they run short of people at the mall, I have to go to Sears and do taxes?' And we just laughed, because we realized for all our slick presentation and business case, we'd missed entirely what was important to our staff people. The answer, of course, was 'No.'"

> *"People were stunned by the news, 'we're going to be owned by H&R Block?' 'Does this mean if they run short of people at the mall, I have to go to Sears and do taxes?'"*

INEVITABLY, CHANGES OCCUR

The Block transaction provided McGladrey with the capital that allowed it to change the way it did acquisitions—fewer deals, but with larger firms and done for cash—and grow faster, said Dan Brooks. Today McGladrey approaches the idea of growth through acquisition in a more targeted manner than it used to. "I think we have a better definition

Knight, Vale and Gregory merged in December 2001 and is now McGladrey's Seattle Economic Unit.

of what we're looking for. I think we have much better systems in place to integrate firms. And I think we're much more aware of what is going to make something a successful or unsuccessful acquisition."

And acquire it has: In the years following the deal with Block, "We were out acquiring firms to help us grow," Travis said. The ability to acquire selectively allowed McGladrey to immediately enter into many of the top-forty markets. "We're in cities like Seattle, Kansas City, Dallas, Washington D.C., Boston, Philadelphia—a number of places where we simply didn't have a presence before," said Travis. "We were able to get presence by using the capital that Block helped provide to acquire firms in those markets."

Chapter 3: A Bold Leap Forward (1999-Present)

> We have a long way to go in the space race. We started late. But **this is the new ocean**, and I believe the United States must **sail on it and be in a position second to none.**
> President John F. Kennedy, 1962

a message from the CEO

Our mission is to be the premier business services firm meeting the needs of middle-market clients. This is a new ocean for RSM McGladrey and McGladrey & Pullen, but an ocean I'm convinced we must sail on. And, like our country's quest to be number one in the space race, our organization can be second to none when it comes to serving mid-sized businesses.

So where are we today? How much closer are we to achieving this goal than we were a year ago? On the financial front, 2001-02 was not a stellar year. While several of our economic units made plans, many fell short. Revenues grew by only 3 percent in a tumultuous year for our country, U.S. businesses and the CPA profession. For more details about our financial performance, refer to Doug Opheim's financial update included later in this report.

In the future, we need to consistently deliver 15 percent revenue growth and 20 percent profit increases. While some of this will come through acquisitions, clearly a substantial portion must come from internal growth through new clients and expanded services to existing clients. This year we must demonstrate our ability to deliver a wide range of services to our client base. In addition to growing revenue through acquisitions, we must create value. As we acquire specialty consulting practices, we need to fully integrate these services into our local practices to successfully transform our Firm and to meet our clients' needs. RSM EquiCo, MBS and Wealth Management are good examples. Challenge yourself to introduce our new services to your clients this year.

We have taken significant steps to integrate firms that joined us following our business combination with H&R Block. We have named new leaders in Kansas City and Philadelphia who are committed to helping us fulfill our vision, and we've consolidated our locations in New York and Chicago.

Last year we added some outstanding firms, like Knight Vale & Gregory, which expanded our presence to the Pacific Northwest. We also strengthened our presence in several key markets with add-on mergers in Florida, Dallas, Milwaukee (Chicago) and Connecticut (New York). The addition of O'Rourke Sacher & Moulton strengthened our already excellent position as leaders in the financial institutions industry.

We've strengthened our management team, adding national leaders in Tax, Manufacturing and Marketing. We're already seeing the results of their efforts in areas such as our expanding State and Local Tax practice, our branding initiative, consulting practice aids, strategic alliances, such as the addition of Mass Mutual to our insurance alliance, and an acquisition that added depth to our Retirement Resources group (formerly MPACT). For more information about these efforts to transform our Firm, refer to the senior management reports on the following pages.

As you know, we have raised the performance bar to ensure we are developing future leaders who can help generate long-term growth and profits. To help develop our leaders, we've committed to providing training to teach the skills needed to be successful and meet personal objectives. And we've introduced a new incentive compensation plan so that our best performers are rewarded for their contributions. Creating a secure future based

A message from Tom Rotherham, CEO, 2002

on steady and consistent growth will assure our more than 4,500 people they can achieve their career goals at RSM McGladrey and McGladrey & Pullen.

We've laid the foundation this year for our external brand roll out. Our brand promise, *Practical Insights, Inspired Results*, captures the essence of the organization we're becoming. Our new tagline, "We See It," is the phrase we'll use to express this promise externally. When our clients face obstacles to their success, we see opportunities to solve the problems they face. Together with our client's management team, we stay focused on the company's vision for growth. To build our brand externally, we need to consistently demonstrate through outstanding client service how we deliver on our brand promise.

We're in the early stages of a transformation of significant magnitude. The foundation has been laid. The success of this transformation rests in your hands and mine, as managing directors in this organization. Major internal transformation rarely happens unless everyone in an organization is involved, beginning with its leadership. **Our ingenuity, creativity and ability to approach the future with eager and open minds will inspire our people to do likewise.**

Tom Rotherham, chief executive officer

Tom Rotherham, CEO

Chapter 3: A Bold Leap Forward (1999-Present)

A leadership team retreat in September 2001. Standing: Bill Travis, Doug Opheim, Duane Tyler, Kathy Kenny. Sitting: Mike Kirley, Tom Rotherham, Bob Jensen.

As a result of its increased presence around the country, McGladrey also is becoming a more recognized name on college campuses and in company boardrooms. It has many more capabilities from a technical standpoint and greater resources from a technological one. "So the basic foundation and reasons for doing the transaction with Block have certainly been very positive," said Travis.

By necessity, McGladrey's governance has become more centralized. "The Block acquisition has brought a level of discipline and management to us that was necessary," said Bob Wilson. "We were growing to a point where we had about 400 partners, and it was much harder to get things done without a corporate structure."

Steve Tait joined the company as president and chief executive officer of RSM McGladrey in 2003. "I had the interesting challenge of being the first person to head the company that wasn't chosen by the board, because I was recruited by H&R Block. My goal really was to blend the best of the partnership world with best practices from the corporate world—bring those two environments together," he said. "I also am the first non-accountant ever to run the firm, which I don't know if that scared everyone to death or gave them all a big sigh of relief," he laughed. "Probably somewhere in between."

Tait's task was to get the company growing and introduce a more professional business management process into the organization, with the goal of getting the entire organization aligned around a common set of objectives: "managing the business for the result we expect to get rather than just trying to do a great job and hoping that something good happens at the end of it," he said. "We are a $1.5 billion organization now—we're not a small accounting firm anymore—and you need professional business practices to manage that. One of the big exciting parts of my job is blending the need for that kind of stuff with the entrepreneurial flair that's created in this sort of decentralized partnership model. I still believe that entrepreneurial spirit is an incredible dynamic in our organization, but we need to be able to sort of put it alongside and merge it into an overall professional business practice."

In 2004 McGladrey achieved double-digit growth in the top and bottom lines, "the first time we'd done that for many years," said Tait. "And we have sustained that performance ever since. That was an important milestone, because firms that don't grow are in danger of not being a firm in the future, and firms that grow create more opportunities for their people, from both a career and personal perspective."

McGladrey & Pullen Board of Directors in 2001 (clockwise from left): Don Natenstedt, John Sanders, Jay Zack, Jeff Canon, Gary Kramer, and Bill Travis

Executive Management Committee in 2001: Jim Blayney, Tom Rotherham, Steve Bauer, Dan Brooks, Bob Lindeman, Gordon Opland, and Pat Murphy

Chapter 3: A Bold Leap Forward (1999-Present)

FOR IMMEDIATE RELEASE

Five New Firms Join RSM McGladrey, McGladrey & Pullen, bringing the goal of a national firm closer

[2000] RSM McGladrey, Inc. and McGladrey & Pullen, LLP, grew considerably in August.

In that month, four of H&R Block's foundation firms and a McGladrey Network firm became part of RSM McGladrey and McGladrey & Pullen, adding hundreds of new employees and thousands of new clients.

"These new firms will help to execute our strategy of becoming a truly national firm," said Bob Jensen, senior vice president, Mergers and Transition. "They will strengthen RSM McGladrey and McGladrey & Pullen by bringing us new ideas, new services, and new, talented people who can see things from a different angle and give us a fresh look at how we do our work."

The new offices give RSM McGladrey a presence in six more top-twenty U.S. markets. The foundation firms added to RSM McGladrey include C.W. Amos & Company of Baltimore, with an office in Bethesda, Maryland, and its affiliate, Turner Pension Consultants, in Annapolis, Maryland; Donnelly Meiners Jordan Kline P.C. (DMJK) of Kansas City, Missouri, with its affiliate GRA, Thompson, White & Co., in Englewood, Colorado; Rudolph Palitz of Blue Bell, Pennsylvania, in suburban Philadelphia, with an office in Cherry Hill, New Jersey; and Wallace Sanders & Co. of Dallas, with an office in Las Colinas, Texas.

The McGladrey Network firm member joining RSM McGladrey is Mallen & Co. of Burlington, Massachusetts, in suburban Boston.

The attest services of each firm have integrated with McGladrey & Pullen, while the non-attest services integrated with RSM McGladrey.

Jensen said the new offices are located in prime markets for growth. "RSM McGladrey now has a solid presence in key cities and can create a powerhouse serving mid-sized businesses that will sustain the firm's continued growth," he said.

The new practices merged with RSM McGladrey for a variety of reasons, but a few are common to all firms: access to national resources, improved continuing professional education (CPE) and employee career advancement opportunities, and a compatibility with the firm's core belief in the value of people, both employees and clients.

Steve Dooley, managing partner, Burlington, Massachusetts, said his office hopes to tap RSM McGladrey's financial institutions' knowledge to develop a small community bank client base. In addition, his office's twelve-member Integrated Technology staff is looking forward to using the firm's wider IT capabilities.

"We have a lot of opportunities in Massachusetts—particularly with community banks—that we haven't been able to capitalize on because we haven't had the resources," said Dooley. "With RSM McGladrey, we'll have those resources."

In exchange, each of the firms brings RSM McGladrey and McGladrey & Pullen its own valuable contribution. Wallace Sanders has growing practices in real estate consulting and international business that it hopes can be of value firmwide. DMJK excels at business valuation, especially financial institutions, and Mullen is widely known for its excellent work with nonprofit organizations, particularly health care and higher education institutions.

The new firms share the same philosophy as RSM McGladrey and McGladrey & Pullen in that they don't try to be all things to all clients.

"We pick only a handful of industries and focus on those, and that part of our message isn't going to change," said Dave Enenbach, managing director, Kansas City.

The new members of the firm report that clients have largely reacted positively to the integration.

Jensen said the latest mergers are a sign of things to come for the firm.

"I know a lot of people expected us to start acquiring new firms a long time ago, and it has taken longer than we originally thought," Jensen said. "But with the merger of these five firms, momentum is now on our side."

Jensen said he expects six more firms to join RSM McGladrey and McGladrey & Pullen in the coming months, in such significant markets as Miami, Seattle, New York City, and San Francisco. In addition, Jensen said two more H&R Block foundation firms in Chicago and Buffalo, New York, are expected to join soon.

They will join Toback CPA of Phoenix, Toback Technology Group of Denver, Human Resources Group of San Diego, and Berg, DeMarco, Lewis, Sawatski & Co. of Chicago, which joined the firm earlier this year.

"It's amazing the number of outstanding firms out there that are talking to us and are excited about joining RSM McGladrey and McGladrey & Pullen," Jensen said.

Jensen said the firm encountered stumbling blocks merging with the new firms, but they were expected because this was the first time so many firms joined at the same time. With a little work, he said, the challenges were met.

He also cautioned against expecting smooth sailing now that the firms have joined RSM McGladrey and McGladrey & Pullen.

"Successful mergers don't happen overnight," he said. "Our experience has shown that it can take as long as twenty-four to thirty-six months before the culture of a new firm is fully integrated, but that's another challenge I know we can meet."

Keller Bruner & Company

In December 2000 RSM McGladrey acquired the non-CPA business of Keller Bruner & Company, one of the Washington, D.C. area's largest regional accounting firms. At the same time, McGladrey & Pullen purchased the attest practice. Keller Bruner, with offices in Bethesda and Frederick, Maryland, and Alexandria, Virginia, was previously a member of the McGladrey Network for eleven years—one of the first firms to join the network.

"Our firm formed very strong relationships with McGladrey, and we had an opportunity to get to know a lot of the people in McGladrey and became dependent on them in doing our business," said Mitch Gorochow, former managing partner of Keller Bruner.

"When McGladrey did the Block deal and started its strategy of filling in the holes around the country, given our relationship and the fact that we were similar organizations in terms of culture and the quality of our people, it became natural for McGladrey to approach us as one of the first acquisitions that they wanted to do." Keller Bruner's excellent reputation for serving the needs of closely held, owner-managed businesses, government contractors, financial institutions, and not-for-profits in the Washington, D.C. area provided a strong foundation for building McGladrey's presence in that marketplace.

Charles Keller and Arthur Bruner

Keller Bruner partners Rick Cole, Ray Green, Mr. Bruner, Mitch Gorochow, and Charles Ballou

Acquiring TBS

The company hit another huge milestone in its development in 2005, when RSM McGladrey purchased the Tax & Business Services (TBS) division of American Express, and McGladrey & Pullen acquired its audit and assurance practice. Established in 1985, TBS was the seventh-largest accounting firm in the United States, with 2004 revenues of $385 million. It marketed its services primarily to small and mid-sized companies. TBS was the first national firm acquired by McGladrey and repositioned the firm to be "the real number five as a CPA firm," with more than $1 billion in revenue, said Tom Horne, executive managing director of the Carolinas Economic Unit. With more than 7,000 accounting professionals—an increase in size of about 40 percent—the combined company became the nation's largest tax, accounting, and business services firm focused on serving mid-sized companies.

Steve Tait said the acquisition of American Express Tax & Business Services delivered other important benefits as well. "This combination will make us a leading provider of services in all but a handful of the largest U.S. markets," he said at the time of the deal. "Our increased scale will also allow us to provide more career opportunities to our current as well as prospective employees, making RSM McGladrey an attractive career alternative to the Big 4 firms."

> *"Our increased scale will also allow us to provide more career opportunities to our current as well as prospective employees, making RSM McGladrey an attractive career alternative to the Big 4 firms."*
>
> *– Steve Tait*

Mike Kirley and Doug Opheim, aka the Blues Brothers, at the 2007 Leadership Conference

Chapter 3: A Bold Leap Forward (1999-Present)

Bill Wells, EMD of Desert Southwest, singing with Elvis at the 2006 Leadership Conference

Our 2006 New Partners and Managing Directors – Our Largest Class Ever

As the audience at a 2006 Leadership Conference indicates, becoming a national firm and acquiring the American Express TBS offices significantly increased McGladrey's size.

64 McGladrey: Beyond the Balance Sheet, 1926-2008

Wealth Management

McGladrey began planning for its wealth management line of business in 1998 and officially announced the service to its clients and the public in July 2000. Pat Murphy, executive vice president of Tax Services, assumed the leadership role.

McGladrey's entrance into the investment advisory business was a natural extension of services already provided by the firm. "We have been working with clients for years on business-related issues," said Murphy. "We know and understand our clients, their companies, and their finances better than other financial service providers. Therefore, we are uniquely qualified to provide financial planning, asset allocation, and investment and tax advice services that address a client's entire net worth. And our clients trust us to provide objective assistance in developing plans for diversifying their investments." The initial focus was on insurance solutions, but over the next two years the focus turned to financial planning and asset management.

Clients come predominantly from the firm's high-net-worth individual tax clients and referrals from those clients. "We currently have 2,978 clients with investable assets of $1.2 to $1.5 million," said David Pierce, a 35-year financial services veteran who joined McGladrey in July 2004 as president of Wealth Management.

"The focus is on mid-market companies on the move from $2.5 million to $1 billion in revenue," said Jay Zack, national service line leader for Private Wealth and Tax Advisory Services and a managing director in National Tax. Zack has been a member of McGladrey for twenty-eight years. "The vast majority of these companies are privately held for whom we do tax planning and compliance for most of the ownership teams. To fully serve the financial needs of these clients, we must offer financial planning, risk management, and investment advisory services to complement our CPA/tax services. As clients trust us and our integrity, they prefer to purchase additional wealth management services from us, their trusted financial advisor."

In a recent article in CPA Wealth Provider, McGladrey was ranked third among all CPA firms that provide wealth management services.

"Wealth Management is a huge growth opportunity for the firm," said Zack. "The line of business has been growing at about 30 percent the last four years. In the summer of 2002, we had just under $400 million of assets under management. Five years later, we have more than $4 billion!"

"We are and will continue to be the fastest growth line of business at McGladrey," said Pierce.

Goldstein Golub Kessler

Stanley Goldstein

Gerry Golub

Stuart Kessler

When it purchased TBS from American Express, McGladrey made New York accounting firm Goldstein Golub Kessler (GGK) a part of its heritage. GGK was founded on the premise that businesses needed high-quality, technical financial management skills to help run their operations and that business owners want responsive, personal, proactive attention to their fiscal needs. GGK has provided audit and attest services in the metro New York area, nationally and internationally, for more than forty-three years. The firm is a leader in serving hedge funds, broker-dealers, investment partnerships, health care entities, not-for-profits, and many other commercial enterprises. The hedge fund practice is among the leaders in auditing several categories of hedge funds, including U.S. funds, offshore funds, fund-of-funds, and emerging markets funds. GGK was the largest single-office firm in the country, with more than 500 employees and 500 professionals in one office, in midtown Manhattan.

GGK has deep roots in New York, where Stanley Goldstein founded the firm in 1964. Seven years later, Stanley Goldstein & Company became Goldstein Golub Kessler, reflecting his partnership with fellow Brooklyn natives Gerry Golub and Stuart Kessler. "The three of them all went to Brooklyn College, which is part of the City University system of New York, and they take great pride in the fact that they all came from Brooklyn, from extremely modest beginnings," said Steven Mayer, RSM McGladrey's executive managing director and a former managing partner of GGK. "Stanley was the face of the firm to the outside world. He was a very deep thinker, maybe a philosopher in many ways, and had strong beliefs as to how one should market, network, and service clients," said Mayer. "Gerry was the networker and the one with the philosophy that if you did a good job for your clients, they would refer you to other clients. Stu Kessler ran the tax department and started doing personal financial planning when it was never done before by accountants."

In 1998 American Express Tax and Business Services acquired GGK as its flagship in New York. "At the time, American Express had forty to forty-five accounting firms throughout the United States," said Mayer. By the time RSM McGladrey acquired TBS from American Express in 2005, TBS had grown to encompass about sixty-five firms, "including several large firms like us." The audit practice of GGK remained separate for two more years before being acquired by McGladrey & Pullen.

"GGK's legacy, I believe, will go down in history as being an extraordinarily fast-growing firm," Mayer said. "We were one of the few firms that stressed marketing and selling, that all partners and even senior staff members should go out and network, meet people, and try to generate new business when other accounting firms never even considered doing that."

Altschuler, Melvoin and Glasser

One of the firms brought into the McGladrey fold via the TBS acquisition was Chicago-based Altschuler, Melvoin and Glasser (AM&G). AM&G provided industry-focused audit services to mid-sized private and public companies, including distribution and wholesale companies, educational institutions, manufacturers, food service companies, not-for-profit organizations, associations, and real estate firms.

On October 1, 1923, Harry Altschuler, a professor of accounting at Northwestern University, and two recent graduates of Northwestern, Charles Melvoin and Morris Glaser, formed a general partnership named Altschuler, Melvoin and Glasser CPAs and opened an office in downtown Chicago to engage in the practice of public accounting. Several years later, Melvoin and Glasser continued their education by attending law school and practicing law under the name of Melvoin and Glasser out of the same offices as AM&G.

Charles Melvoin and Morris Glaser

AM&G existed as a single-office practice (recognized as the largest of its kind in the United States) until 1985, when AM&G opened a Los Angeles office. In 1992 AM&G opened a New York office specializing in litigation support and, shortly thereafter, a Washington, D.C. office, and for a short time it maintained a Phoenix office to service the substantial engagements it was receiving from the federal government's Resolution Trust Corporation. In 1993 the firm was reorganized along industry lines, "which we found to be a great driver of profitable growth," said Howard Stone. Stone started his career in public accounting with AM&G shortly after graduating from the University of Illinois in June 1957. He served as AM&G's managing partner from 1982 until 1999, when the tax and consulting practices of the firm were sold to TBS. "AM&G was by far the largest TBS office," he said.

AM&G's attest business, which previously had an alternative practice structure with TBS, was acquired by McGladrey & Pullen in October 2005. As a result of the acquisition, sixty partners and sixty-three directors joined McGladrey & Pullen. When considered together, McGladrey & Pullen, LLP, and RSM McGladrey, Inc., now rank as the third-largest provider of accounting, tax and business consulting services in the Chicago area.

AM&G brought to McGladrey a large group of highly trained personnel indoctrinated to perform quality services in the tradition of "super-pleasing" clients. Additionally, AM&G brought special expertise in the real estate industry, litigation support services, and other professional service areas.

"Merger involves change, which is always difficult," said Stone, who "saw a great similarity between McGladrey and AM&G with its Midwest-based culture, work ethic, and high integrity." "However, when the parties share cultural and professional similarities, the change is more easily accomplished."

Changes Resulting from a Bold Leap Forward
(1999-2008)

- 5,000 More Employees

- 18 vs. 7 of the Top 25 Markets

- Advanced our Specialized Service Capabilities – Technology Risk Management Services, International Tax, State and Local Tax, Wealth Management, Capital Markets

- Birth of Functional Leadership

- Expanded and Standardized Partner Expectations

- Go-to-Market Growth Culture in EUs

- Initiated National Marketing Campaigns

- Improved HR Management

- Implemented Real Time Financial Reporting (EMERGE)

- Established Formal Managing for Results Process

Chapter Four

Creating Our Future

(2008 AND BEYOND)

> "We are in a strong position to win the middle market— a $35 billion market opportunity."
>
> *- Steve Tait*

The middle market, which itself continues to evolve, remains McGladrey's key focus. The midsized company "truly is the heart of U.S. commerce and industry," said Steve Tait, with more than 500,000 businesses contributing more than 30 percent of the nation's GDP and representing one-third of all American workers. "We are in a strong position to win the middle market— a $35 billion market opportunity. McGladrey already leads mid-tier competitors in middle-market share, and our unique blend of local resources coupled with deep national industry expertise continues to differentiate our firm. The Big 4 are deep into this space, but we can become the Big 1 for the middle market by staying focused on our clients' unique needs and aspirations while providing a high level of personalized service."

In the global market, today's middle-market clients are more likely to have ownership that comes from a foreign country, a private equity firm, or a diverse group of shareholders. "They're much more likely to have multiple locations, to have outsourced manufacturing to overseas, to have formed strategic relationships or foreign subsidiaries, and to operate in multiple locations in multiple countries," said Dave Scudder. "So as those clients are no longer tied to geography, our firm needs to be able to respond to that and be able to work across geographic boundaries, nationally and internationally."

"The clients we serve are closely held businesses, or operate as if they are closely held," said Mike Kirley. "We get so close to the owner, the shareholders, and the employees that the relationships become in a very unique way, a combination of

Focused on Midsized Manufacturers

Manufacturing and wholesale distribution represent the largest base of clients served by McGladrey, which provides services to more than 8,000 manufacturers, wholesalers, and distributors in industries as diverse as food processing and distribution, printing and publishing, metal fabrication, and electronic and electrical equipment.

McGladrey produces an annual manufacturing and wholesale distribution national survey in order to provide valuable information to midsized companies across the United States.

In the spring of 2007, McGladrey surveyed manufacturers and wholesale distributors across the United States. This second annual nationwide survey was designed to assess what CEOs, CFOs, and other senior industry executives were thinking, doing, and planning to grow their businesses in an increasingly competitive marketplace. Participants were asked questions about cost structure, profitability, technology initiatives, operations, globalization, and more. Research captured in this report highlights national and regional trends among all survey participants, providing unique findings on the condition of specific industry segments. With these report findings, company executives and industry leaders are better positioned to examine a range of factors impacting this industry.

Tedder, James, Worden & Associates

One of McGladrey's most recent acquisitions was Orlando-based Tedder, James, Worden & Associates, in June 2007.

"We started Tedder, James, Worden & Associates in July 1997 and operated the first four years without any association with McGladrey," said Johnnie James, the firm's former manager partner. "However, we soon realized that as we grew, we needed more national and international resources to be able to support our growing client base and their diverse needs. We also needed to develop better HR tools to help us evaluate and develop our staff."

Tedder, James, Worden chose to join the McGladrey Network. "Over the following six years we sent staff to McGladrey training sessions, we attended annual McGladrey Network partner meetings, we attended biannual managing partner round tables, etc.," James said. "As a firm, we also decided to adopt McGladrey's paperless audit methodology and utilize the same tax processing platform as McGladrey. Thus, we were very aligned with McGladrey on the core service tools and HR systems. The HR and strategic support we received from McGladrey allowed us to stay focused on the marketplace and grow our practice at an accelerated rate. McGladrey became a big part of who we were and was a key part of our marketing. As a result, we grew our firm from 5 people in July 1997 to 110 people in June 2007." Tedder, James, Worden became the second-largest accounting firm in central Florida.

"I happened to be in Chicago for a McGladrey Managing Partner Leadership Conference in mid-October 2006 when Dan Brooks asked me if I would join him for dinner to 'catch up,' as he wanted to share with me some things McGladrey had going on in Florida. At dinner Dan shared the Florida vision of becoming a $100 million EU within four years but said they could not reach that goal without an office in Orlando. He shared that McGladrey would prefer that Tedder, James, Worden become that office. However, he also stated that if we did not join the firm, he believed that they would establish an Orlando office without us within the next three years and he was unsure where that would leave us relative to the Network. Given our strong reliance on the McGladrey Network and the challenge of replacing that support, it was clear to me that we needed to seriously consider formally joining McGladrey." In December of that year, the equity partners of Tedder, James, Worden voted unanimously to accept McGladrey's offer.

business and personal. We have been able to maintain that even as we become a more growth-oriented firm, and I think that speaks well for us and I think it speaks a lot about the markets we serve. They're interested in relationships as opposed to projects. Instead of saying, 'I buy my tax services from McGladrey' or 'my audit services from McGladrey & Pullen,' they're interested in having that relationship. In other words, they look to McGladrey as a key part of their success."

"We have the ability to serve really complex, strong, entrepreneurial middle-market organizations, and they're starting to see that," said Mitch Gorochow, executive managing director for the Mid-Atlantic Economic Unit.

"A real strength of McGladrey that existed when I came here and persists today is the entrepreneurial spirit," said Kirley. "We look for our people to take chances, we look for our people to be innovative and try something new. It's okay here to take a shot at something and have it turn out less than perfect. The important part was that you tried something new; you saw a need and you tried to fill it."

One of McGladrey's newer efforts has involved the presence of its 'business developers." In 2004 the firm had no more than five full-time outside sales personnel. In an effort to accelerate growth and create a growth culture, a national sales organization was created. Rod Riemann, Director of Business Development – Upper Midwest Economic Unit, was in the initial group of eight sales professionals hired. Reflecting on the growth of the sales organization, Reimann indicated, "We've now grown to over forty full-time business developers throughout the firm. The first couple of years were quite an adjustment. Accepting full-time sales professionals required a change in the culture. Now we are an integral part of the team."

> *"We have the ability to serve really complex, strong, entrepreneurial middle-market organizations, and they're starting to see that," said Mitch Gorochow, executive managing director for the Mid-Atlantic Economic Unit.*

McGladrey Culture

McGladrey's culture has always been one of its greatest strengths. "I believe a key reason we're here today is because of the culture that was created and has grown out of Iowa," said Tait, citing traditional Midwestern values of social responsibility, caring for one another, integrity, trust. "I guess everyone talks about those things but you don't have to spend many days in the McGladrey environment to know that those values really do exist in our organization."

From that culture springs McGladrey's approach to building the best workforce. "We've learned that we can't sit still for a moment in our efforts to attract, develop, and retain the right talent. By the 'right' talent, I mean those who are professionally challenged and intellectually stimulated by our clients and their business challenges," said Kimpa Moss, chief human resources officer. "We have to stay ahead of the demands of our employees and our clients – by continually evolving our approach. An example of the evolution in our approach includes our focus on work/life strategies to better help our employees meet both their professional and their personal commitments. We've also invested in advancing the career paths of women, in building programs and benefits that support our employees in their personal lives, and in creating flexibility in when, where, and how we do our work."

Diane McNulty commented on the evolution of one of the programs originally designed to retain more women in the profession and in the firm. "What began as a strategy to retain more women at higher levels, however, has become a demand of changing generations of employees, regardless of gender. Work/life balance issues are not a concern for just the women of McGladrey, but for all its current and potential employees. They know if we are going to attract the best people, we need to have a flexible work arrangement, and I think they do a wonderful job for all of us."

Attracting and retaining its employees is not a bold leap for McGladrey. Dan Trigg, pictured with Kimpa Moss and Marla Becker in 1997, was recognized during the 1998 Partners Meeting for mentoring these 2 new partners.

Chapter 4: Creating Our Future (2008 and Beyond)

Human Resources

The function of human resources for the firm has evolved tremendously through the years. McGladrey learned a great deal by trial and error when it was growing through frequent mergers, particularly in the late 1970s and early 1980s. Gradually, professionally trained and certified human-resource professionals were brought into the fold, and today McGladrey strikes a balance between its professional HR personnel and those who have come from the client services side of the business.

McGladrey's chief human resources officer, Kimpa Moss, said, "I feel strongly about HR both supporting and modeling our core values and equipping the firm for what comes next with our workforce," citing employee development, a flexible work environment, and emphasis on career coaching. "The most important linkage is aligning our client service approach and requirements with the needs, aspirations and development of our people.

Today, said Bob Wilson, a former national Human Resources director and currently Human Resources director for the New York practice, "Our approach is much more along the lines of a talent development business, and we look at ourselves as a place where not only can clients get great service, but our people can gain unparalleled experience by coming to work with us."

People and their development have always been an important part of the history of McGladrey, which was recognized with awards from *Working Mother* in 2006 and 2007.

Jennifer Kalla, working on tax returns with her husband, Paul, at their home, went to check on son Ethan when she heard him crying. The Kallas are both CPAs in McGladrey's Minneapolis office, where Jennifer negotiated a flexible schedule to help them juggle work and family.

The *Working Mother* Gala dinner at the Sheraton Hotel in New York City in 2006. RSM McGladrey was recognized by the magazine as one of the best 100 companies to work for. Pictured, left to right, are Patty Blackburn, Teresa Hopke, Lisa Seaman Anderson, and Gerry Golub.

In January 2008, McGladrey recognized its HR professionals for their commitment to the company's people philosophy: character, commitment, competence, and one-firm contribution. Top row: Kimpa Moss, Michelle McKenzie, Joe Bellavary, Mary Maguire, Alisa Brussel, Nicole Roberge, Dave Swinehart, Ken Bansemer, Sherley Bowen, and Robin Palchus. Bottom row: Amanda Turcotte, Lauren Suarez, Julie Becker, Becky Melton, and Tiffany Hansen.

Chapter 4: Creating Our Future (2008 and Beyond)

In Central Plains EU, May 1, 2008

The unanimous Declaration by our partners and managing directors of a
Flexible Work Environment

When, in the course of human events, it becomes necessary for the employees of the Central Plains Economic Unit of RSM McGladrey Inc. and McGladrey and Pullen to meet the needs of their clients, to successfully pursue their career goals, and to achieve the business goals set forth by our stakeholders, and at the same time be able to lead happy and fulfilling personal lives, all must unite with one accord and declare that this will be a work environment of flexibility.

We hold these truths to be self-evident, that a successful career with RSM McGladrey Inc. and McGladrey and Pullen demands hard work, long hours, and an unwavering commitment to serving our clients needs. That success begins with personal accountability and dedication to doing that which needs to be done. That at times this will require personal sacrifice, putting long range goals before short term rewards. That employees' ability to achieve an appropriate balance in their lives and live fully is positive for the business.

A work environment where all will have the flexibility to balance the needs of work and personal lives demands that each person is personally accountable for meeting client needs and business goals. That freely sharing information regarding assignments, schedules, and client needs is essential to operating in a flexible environment. That employees will be judged by and rewarded for results, not actions. That face-time serves no noble purpose. That each person takes responsibility for balancing their time, completing their work and communicating essential information to others. That the personal needs and differences of each individual be respected and supported by all. That employees can feel safe to discuss their life balance needs with their co-workers and leaders without reprisal.

We, therefore, the partners and managing directors of the Central Plains Economic Unit, assembled, do, in the name, and by the authority of the good people of our EU, solemnly publish and declare, that we will support a flexible work environment. And for the support of this declaration, with a firm reliance on the protection of Divine Providence, we mutually pledge to each other our lives, our fortunes and our sacred honor.

As we go to press, here is a creative way one EU is considering implementing the flexible work environment for their employees. This declaration will be owned by the partners and managing directors in that EU to demonstrate true commitment to a flexible work environment.

English 101

Professional development at RSM McGladrey can take many forms. But in the Dallas EU, hiring an English tutor may be a first-of-its-kind opportunity to help employees excel at their jobs.

According to Executive Managing Director Roger Hendren, an employee of Chinese descent was turning in average performance—not because he wasn't good at his job, but simply because he lacked a command of the English language.

"It's so hard to attract and keep good talent these days," said Hendren. "Attempting something that's a little unorthodox is not out of the question."

So Hendren and Byron Whittlinger, human resource director–Dallas, set out to hire an English coach. "I did an Internet search and located about a dozen possible candidates," said Whittlinger. "After narrowing down the list and checking references, I hired someone to tutor certain employees once a week for about two months."

Those English lessons seemed to make all the difference. Michael Guo, the student who took the classes, pointed to testimonials from others that the tutoring was a big success. "My coworkers and clients said my English skills improved a lot. And now I feel more confident and comfortable talking with people. That's the most important thing."

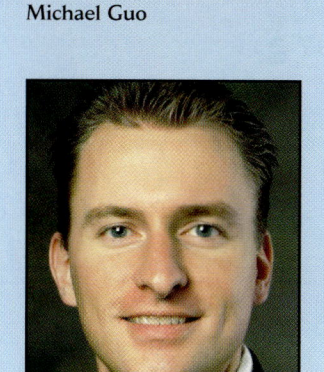

Michael Guo

Byron Whittlinger

As an auditor, Guo knows that communication is key to a successful engagement. "With my increased confidence, I find more opportunities to talk to people. And I know that this communication is more effective and reflects well on my job performance."

According to Hendren, senior-level managers took note of Guo's improved performance, too. "We recently landed a regional grocery store chain as a new client," Hendren said. "I encouraged the two lead client servers to 'pick the best talent' for this project. And in two independent conversations with me, they each requested Michael."

That ringing endorsement speaks volumes for the extra steps the Dallas EU took for its employees' professional development. "Hiring an English coach cost us a few thousand dollars as an EU," Hendren explained. "But if I could spend several thousand of dollars to turn every average performer into a stellar performer, I'd do it every time."

Chapter 4: Creating Our Future (2008 and Beyond)

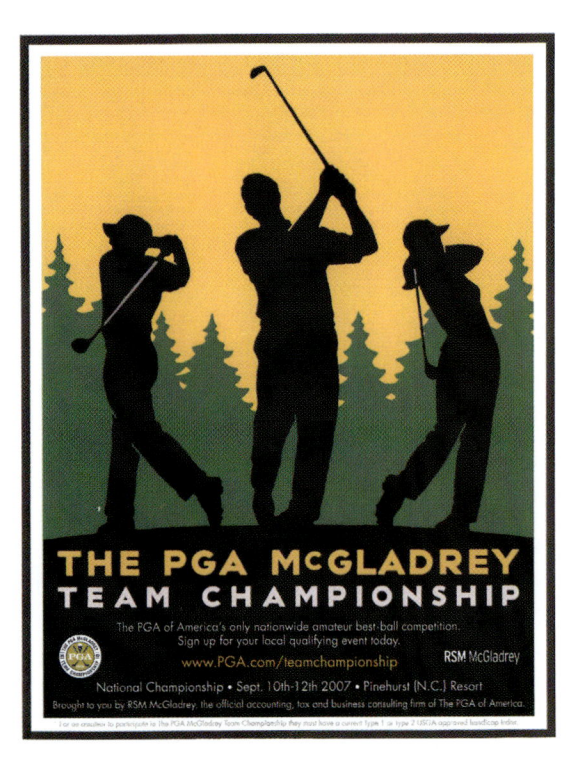

An RSM McGladrey advertisement launching The PGA McGladrey Team Championship was used to help build the company's brand name in specific market niches.

BUILDING A STRONG BRAND POSITION

In addition, McGladrey is proactively managing its brand position, both at home and abroad, said Tait. The McGladrey brand is well-known in the Midwest, but in many of the new metropolitan markets the firm is entering, its name is unfamiliar. "It's directly correlated to the origins of the firm and where it has grown from . . . We are working to build our brand in new markets right now, and it will make a big difference to our business long-term."

"In the past few years, there has been a real focus on building recognition of our brand nationally," said marketing director Connie Smith Benning. "The avenue that we've selected to do that is sports marketing." McGladrey sponsors three professional golfers, Chris DiMarco, Natalie Gulbis, and Zach Johnson, winner of the 2007 Masters tournament.

"In addition to that, we're sponsoring a new PGA event for amateurs," said Smith Benning. The PGA McGladrey Team Championship is the first nationwide amateur tournament managed by the PGA of America in its 92-year history, reflecting the kind of achievement McGladrey strives to make with all its clients. The event features local qualifying events, 41 PGA section championships held throughout the year and a culminating national championship field of 41 four-person teams. Local qualifying events are open to men and women players of all ages and playing abilities with an established handicap. In 2007, the event's first year, the championship took place at North Carolina's famed Pinehurst Resort, where the National Championship returns in 2008. RSM McGladrey is the official accounting, tax, and business consulting firm of The PGA of America, and The PGA McGladrey Team Championship reinforces McGladrey's position as the firm for "companies on the move." It also increases brand awareness in the nearly 100 communities that have RSM McGladrey offices throughout the country.

The PGA McGladrey Team Championship logo

"We're also trying something new this year," said Smith Benning, highlighting some of the company's other brand-building activities in advertising and public relations. In the fall of 2007, McGladrey leveraged its own experts in *Fortune* and on CNNMoney.com to provide answers to middle-market companies. The company also expanded its radio coverage with nationwide advertising on XM Radio and ventured into cable television in several major markets. It has achieved some great media coverage from industry publications like *Accounting Today* and national media like the *Wall Street Journal*. "All of these activities build our brand, showcase our people and expertise, and position us as advocates for the middle market," said Tait.

One of seven CNN Money ads launched in 2007 to expand advertising of RSM McGladrey

Natalie Gulbis, an LPGA tour golfer sponsored by RSM McGladrey

Chris DieMarco, PGA golfer sponsored by RSM McGladrey

Zach Johnson at the 2007 Masters

Chapter 4: Creating Our Future (2008 and Beyond) 79

GLOBAL FUTURE

Today, McGladrey is the largest member in RSM International, contributing about $1.4 billion of the organization's global total of $2.9 billion. "Globalization is a real phenomenon, and the reality is there are both opportunities and significant risks represented to the client base we serve in the United States," said Tait. "Having a strong international capability that better meets their needs is a very key requirement of our U.S. growth strategy, let alone any global aspirations that we may have. We did some research a while back that told us that close to 40 percent of middle-market companies in the United States have interests outside of the United States, mostly in Western Europe, although areas of Asia, such as China, and India, are rapidly growing environments. Today we do serve those requirements for our U.S. clients; the difference is we serve them through other member firms that are part of the international network."

Bill Wells, 1996, thinking about our global future

In order to further improve the delivery of integrated services to its internationally active clients, RSM International has developed an intensive training course for senior personnel. "RSM Academy" was launched in June 2007, when the organization hosted partners and staff from member firms throughout the global network. Senior managers, directors, and junior partners from assurance, tax, and consulting service lines worked together for one week during the residential event near Eindhoven, The Netherlands. The academy helps member firms draw on the strong international links and capabilities within RSM to better serve their cross-border clients and improves the international capabilities of delegates with international programs covering client service, technical, and managerial skills. In addition, it offers RSM's global client servers the opportunity to focus on international issues together.

"We're investing much time and intellectual capital in the RSM Academy to make sure our existing and future international clients are provided with a consistently great service from member firms," said Jean Stephens, CEO of RSM International. "Our clients demand the best from our people. The RSM Academy is part of our global response to ensure we attract, train, and retain the most talented professionals in our markets."

"Today we view international [markets] from the point of view of ensuring we're members of a good network, an international organization that meets the non-U.S. requirements of our U.S. client base," said Tait. "In the future, that would still prevail, but we may look at owning international assets as part of our growth strategy. Our overall priority is to get to a top-five position in the top twenty-five markets in the U.S. But part of doing that is ensuring you have a very strong international capability, and sometimes owning that international capability or parts of it will put you in a stronger position," said Tait. "We want to be a $5 billion-plus organization as quickly as we can, and we can't get there just through organic growth, and perhaps we can't get there just by acquisition growth in the U.S.; you know, we may have to think further afield."

"Globalization is real, and the need to have a strong and robust international capability is a really important element of any accounting firm's growth strategy in the United States."

Chinese and Singapore partners visit St. Louis in May 2007.

The inaugural RSM Academy included fifteen attendees from the United States.

Chapter 4: Creating Our Future (2008 and Beyond)

RSM International

In 1964 McGladrey, Hansen, Dunn & Company was a founding partner of DRM (Dunwoody Robson McGladrey) International, an affiliation of international accounting and consulting firms.

By 1978 its member firms were located in twenty-one countries and had correspondent firms in another twenty countries. Known internationally as Dunwoody Robson McGladrey & Pullen, members of the firm retained their identity and autonomy. The benefits derived from this membership included a sharing of resources between the participating firms and better service to clients due to the advantage of referral work between countries served.

In 1993 it became RSM International. Collectively, it is the seventh-largest international client-service group in public accounting. Today there are about 24,000 people in RSM, in 621 offices in more than seventy countries.

Teaming with an international firm

"The immediate benefit [of membership in RSM International] is to ensure that, as our clients get bigger and more global, we can meet their needs and deliver a service that's consistent with the standards they are used to with us," said Mike Kirley, who serves as chairman of the board of RSM International. "If a client acquires a division in France, now we can use RSM France to provide the services there, and you know by virtue of the fact that they are part of RSM that you are going to get the RSM level of quality. That's quite unique: a lot of international organizations don't have that emphasis on a consistent standard for delivery of service that we do."

"The importance of having an international service capability has increased significantly in the last ten years with McGladrey's rapid growth, and even more so in the last five as we've continued to acquire relationships with larger and larger clients, who are of course more likely to be international."

Jean Stephens pictured with Sabry Heakal, chief executive officer of RSM International

PREPARING THE NEXT GENERATION

Like its peers in the accounting world, McGladrey is looking ahead, well aware how crucial the rising generation of talent is to its future success. "The biggest key to our success going forward is people and our ability to attract and retain them," said Dave Scudder, managing partner of McGladrey & Pullen. Changes in a post-Enron world mean fewer accounting firms and a much higher demand for accounting services, he said. "It's a war for talent."

Fully intending to emerge from that war victorious, McGladrey is concentrating on ways to increase its focus on national recruiting and the utilization of college interns as well as appeal to a generation looking for careers that provide lots of variety and opportunity. Today's generation of young people are very smart about their careers, said Bill Travis. "They want to be challenged, they want to be in a place where they're constantly growing and being mentored, and they want the opportunity to move up the ladder so that they get a high degree of fulfillment out of their work hours."

> "The number-one issue for our people that they would describe as being the most important part of their experience at McGladrey is their understanding of their career development opportunities and the paths they can pursue that enable them to achieve those goals. So we're doing a lot of work in that area." – Steve Tait

McGladrey's 2007 interns: "our future"

Chapter 4: Creating Our Future (2008 and Beyond)

RSM McGladrey Career Day

Interns at the 2007 Summer Capstone Conference

MaP: Your future

Summer interns attend a two-and-a-half-day national conference which focuses on defining and developing their career aspirations. Participants meet their peers from all across the country, and together they work on leadership skills, discuss work/life balance issues, learn about McGladrey culture, and take some time to focus on their long-term development.

The primary challenge facing the firm, Steve Tait said, "is ensuring that we continue to nurture, develop, and continuously improve our employee culture so that we can become increasingly a compelling place to come to work each day, and also become increasingly more attractive to both young people and experienced people who are either interested in becoming a member of the profession or are already in the profession."

"The number-one issue for our people that they would describe as being the most important part of their experience at McGladrey is their understanding of their career development opportunities and the paths they can pursue that enable them to achieve those goals. So we're doing a lot of work in that area."

McGladrey will definitely be around to see its 100th birthday, Tait said, "and it will make a lot more years beyond that. It had some humble beginnings, and Ira McGladrey would probably be stunned if he knew what his organization had become, but we are here to stay. I do believe we will make a very real difference in the success of middle-market companies in the United States, because we have a very strong foundation both culturally and with our people. I think that will continue to serve us well into the future."

The New Class

Katie Bushard started work in Chicago as an associate consultant in risk management, her first job out of college, in September 2007. She shared a few thoughts at the end of her first week on the job:

- *Why McGladrey?* "I grew up in Minnesota, where McGladrey is a familiar name in the business community. I also went to college in the Twin Cities, so McGladrey became even more visible to me and when the time came, it seemed like a great career option for me."

- *Class of '07:* "Our class [of new hires in the Great Lakes region] is eighty-four people, which is the biggest starting class in this EU McGladrey has ever had. It's fun because although I won't be working closely with all of my start class, I automatically have this network of friends and colleagues who are experiencing many of the same things I am as a young professional."

- *Feeling at home:* "It's a very professional atmosphere—everyone is obviously here to provide services to our clients—but there seems to be a very friendly, family-like atmosphere within the firm, too."

Katie Bushard

- *When training is over:* "I'm most excited to start work, to actually be on a project at a client with my team, working on something . . . I feel like I just want to be let go, run and do it and see how it goes."

- *McGladrey on TV:* "I am an avid golfer and fan of the game, so I love the fact that McGladrey is using golf as a platform to build our brand. I follow the PGA and LPGA week to week, and for me it's a source of pride to see 'McGladrey' on the hats and shirts of our sponsored players. It was so exciting to see Zach Johnson win the Masters this year. I think his victory will continue to be something people inside and outside our firm are proud of and associate with McGladrey. I told everyone, Hey, that guy won the Masters—that's my company!'"

- *Looking ahead:* "McGladrey continues to grow internationally, and that is something that attracted me to the company, because I would love to work abroad or travel abroad for work someday. Knowing international opportunities exist within the company and that there will continue to be more of these opportunities is very exciting to me."

Steve Tait

I'm a big fan of history. As the president of the fifth-largest tax, accounting, and business-consulting firm in the country, I think it's just as important to know where you've been as it is to envision where you're going.

That's why I believe it's necessary to appreciate the contributions of our founder, Ira B. McGladrey, and the partners and employees who've made McGladrey what it is today.

Our corporate values are respect, integrity, teamwork, client focus, and excellence. These values helped form the culture that Ira McGladrey established for the firm he founded in 1926, and they still accurately reflect how we work and serve our clients today.

It's reassuring to know that RSM McGladrey's foundation remains the same. Even as we face very different challenges today, such as demanding segmentation, niche industry needs, and globalization, we continue to serve middle-market clients with commitment and honesty through strong, trusted relationships.

We owe a lot to our history and the contributions of those who came before us. With our success, however, I believe Ira McGladrey would be proud.

Regards,
Steve Tait
President, RSM McGladrey

Business failures and scandals. Capital markets and the wildly fluctuating economy. The U.S. government scrambling to make accounting and tax rules in response to these difficult business conditions.

Sound familiar? The events that we live with today were just as relevant in 1926 when Ira B. McGladrey, an Iowa accountant, founded what is known today as McGladrey & Pullen, LLP. Mr. McGladrey, his partners, and his employees were dedicated – like we are today – to serving the accounting and tax needs of middle-market clients.

Dave Scudder

Middle America was a fitting birthplace for a firm focused on the needs of middle-market businesses. Guiding principles of integrity, expertise, and personal service were scaled to a business model focused on the middle market. Our clients then, as now, demanded assistance from a CPA firm that not only knew the rules but knew how to help clients understand and apply those rules to their own business.

A culture of attention to detail and an unwavering focus on the middle market has served McGladrey & Pullen for more than eighty years. While the headlines and glamour often go to bigger companies and bigger accounting firms, the middle market has always known where to turn for guidance and integrity. I'm very proud to have been a part of this firm for more than twenty years and for the privilege of holding the position of managing partner.

Today our firm employs more than 600 partners and 8,000 employees from coast to coast. Our name has changed through the years as we've added new people and locations and made several significant acquisitions and mergers. But the constant through all of those changes has been the values of the people we bring in and the devotion to serving the needs of the middle market with the same integrity and dedication that our founding partners had. Our success has always been measured by the success of our people and our clients. And on that score, I'm certain we've been a winner.

I hope that you enjoy this history of our firm and the stories of those who've helped us on our journey. Our current partners are the placeholders for future generations of partners and employees as they take this firm to greater heights and further success. This book represents a tribute to those who came before us, and those who shaped and positioned our firm for that future. We thank them for their guidance and for the lessons they taught us as we navigate through today's business challenges.

Thanks!
Dave Scudder
Managing Partner, McGladrey & Pullen, LLP

Appendix One

How Our EUs Were Built Through Mergers

This appendix is a summary of how the current Economic Unit (EU) structure was built through mergers. It includes mergers (other than single practices) since the office merged into McGladrey. Mergers prior to that have not been included. The year listed is the year that the office was merged (and closed, where applicable). If available, the actual years that the predecessor firm or office was in existence are noted in parentheses.

Year	Office	Merger or Other
BOSTON		
2000	Burlington, MA	Mullen & Co.
2005	Quincy, MA	TBS–Ziner, Kennedy & Lehan LLP
2005	Boston, MA	TBS–Ziner, Kennedy & Lehan LLP
BUFFALO FMSM		
2000	Buffalo, NY	Freed, Maxick & Battaglia (Not M&P)
		HRB–Freed Maxick Sachs and Murphy (Not M&P)
2000	Batavia, NY	HRB–Battaglia Andrews & Moag (Not M&P)
2007	Rochester, NY	Bernardi & Russo (Not M&P)
CAROLINAS		
1984	Raleigh, NC	A.M. Pullen & Company (1912–1984)
1984	Greensboro, NC	A.M. Pullen & Company (1929–1984)
1984–2000	Winston-Salem, NC	A.M. Pullen & Company (1938–1984)
1984–2001	Harrisonburg, VA	A.M. Pullen & Company (1942–1984)
1984	Charlotte, NC	A.M. Pullen & Company (1946–1984)

Appendixes

Year	Office	Merger or Other
CAROLINAS *(continued)*		
1984–1986	Atlanta, GA	A.M. Pullen & Company (1955–1984)
1984	New Bern, NC	A.M. Pullen & Company (1961–1984)
1984–1986	Columbia, SC	A.M. Pullen & Company (1963–1984)
1984–1985	Knoxville, TN	A.M. Pullen & Company (1968–1984)
1984–1990	Asheville, NC	A.M. Pullen & Company (1975–1984)
1984–1986	Winchester, VA	A.M. Pullen & Company (1977–1984)
1984–1985	Danville, VA	A.M. Pullen & Company (1977–1984)
1984	Moorehead City, NC	A.M. Pullen & Company (1978–1984)
1984–1995	Hickory, NC	A.M. Pullen & Company (1978–1984)
1984–1985	Memphis, TN	A.M. Pullen & Company (1979–1984)
1984	Shelby, NC	A.M. Pullen & Company (1979–1984)
1984	Rocky Mount, NC	A.M. Pullen & Company (1980–1984)
1984–1987	Fayetteville, NC	A.M. Pullen & Company (1981–1984)
1984–1988	Norfolk, VA	A.M. Pullen & Company (1983–1984)
1984	Greenville, NC	Edwards & Clark, PA
1992	Wilmington, NC	Lowrimore, Warwick & Company (1941–1992)

Year	Office	Merger or Other
CENTRAL MIDWEST		
1969	Springfield, IL	Whitney, Hakman & Conaghan
		Randy Ragan (Former Deloitte & Touche Office) (1970–1998)
1971	Peoria, IL	Morgan, Ellis & Co. and Krieger, Greiner & Allovio (1937–1971)
1978	Galesburg, IL	Tobin & Clark (1954–1978)
		KPMG Main Hurdman (1987)
1982	Champaign, IL	Winakor, Bates & Brunson, PC (1955–1982)
		Filbey, Summers & Co (1928–1982)
2004	St. Louis, MO	Established

Year	Office	Merger or Other
CENTRAL PLAINS		
1926	Cedar Rapids, IA	Billings, Prouty and Tompkins
		Bell & Van Zee P.C. (1992)
1926	Davenport, IA	Billings, Prouty and Tompkins
		KMPG (1991)
1927	Burlington, IA	Expansion
1933	Iowa City, IA	Expansion

Year	Office	Merger or Other

Central Plains *(continued)*

Year	Office	Merger or Other
1939–1942	Omaha, NE	
1945	Des Moines, IA	Boyer Berthoff & Co.
		McClure & Co. (1965)
		Martin, Lees, Fardel and Newell (1975)
		Alexander Grant & Co. (1981)
		Hamilton & Associates (1992)
		Coopers and Lybrand (1995)
		Humiston, Skokan, Warren and Eichenberger (1968–2000)
		Flood & Youngers (1992–2000)
1950–1983	Rock Island, IL	Established
1955–1992	Marshalltown, IA	R.A. Wester & Co.
1955–1991	Fort Dodge, IA	Established
1957	Dubuque, IA	Established
		Pink & Kolf (1972)
1959–1985	Iowa Falls, IA	Edgar S. Gage & Co.
1959	Mason City, IA	Edgar S. Gage & Co.
1947–1994	Clinton, IA	Established
1973	Waterloo, IA	Established
		James Barren, CPA (1978)
		Don McCombs & Associates (1979)
		R.A. Snyder & Associates (1986)
1949–1975	Keokuk, IA	Established
1953–2004	Moline, IL	Established
1972–2000	Casper, WY	Raab, Roush & Gaymon
		Tangrey, Harris & Homer (1981)
		Shamley and Kilmer (1989)
1972–2000	Cheyenne, WY	Raab, Roush & Gaymon
		Townsend, Phillips & Co.
1978–1983	Ames, IA	Established
1978–1996	Denver, CO	Broeker Hendrickson & Co. (1977–1978)
		Brown, Whitely and Todd (1980)
		Zaveral, Boosalis and Raisch (1980)
		Newman & Company (1967–1983)
		McGough, Kramer & Co. P.C. (1976–1988)
1986–1999	Sterling, CO	Pyle & Associates
1986–1988	Boulder, CO.	Legerski, Dooley & Company
1986–1994	Ft. Morgan, CO	Merger

Year	Office	Merger or Other
CENTRAL PLAINS *(continued)*		
1986–1991	Laramie, WY	Brolyer & Company P.C.
		Simonsen, Mader & Company (1989)
1999	Denver, CO	Toback Technology Group of Denver
2000	Kansas City, MO	HRB–Donnelly Meiners Jordan Kline P.C.
		HRB–Sigman Page Curry (1998)
		HRB–Troupe Kehoe (1998)
		HRB–GRA, Thompson, White & Co. (1998)
2006	Omaha, NE	Established
DALLAS		
2000	Dallas, TX	HRB–Wallace Sanders & Co.
		HRB - Kinder & Wyman (2000)
		Fisk Robinson & Co. (1969–2001)
DESERT SOUTHWEST		
1978	Las Vegas, NV	Harmon and Company
		Grant Thornton (1987)
1980–1988	Reno, NV	Chanslor, Barbieri & DeWhitt (Separate EU)
1987	Phoenix, AZ	Schulman, Klock & Co., P.C. (1961–1987)
		Toback CPA (2000)
		TBS–Altschuler, Melvoin & Glasser, LLP, Arizona (2005)
		Gaughan & Nahom (2006)
1987–1993	Mesa, AZ	Schulman, Klock & Co., P.C. (1961–1987)
FLORIDA		
1984	Ft Lauderdale, FL	A.M. Pullen & Company (1982–1984)
		Pannel Kerr Forster (1988)
		TBS–Millward and Company, Inc. (2005)
1984	Gainesville, FL	A.M. Pullen & Company (1978–1984)
1988	West Palm Beach, FL	Pannel Kerr Forster
1992	Naples, FL	Established
		How, Cacchione Gainey PA (2000)
2003	Miami, FL	Bustamante, Nunez & Company (2003)

Year	Office	Merger or Other

FLORIDA (continued)

2005	Melbourne, FL	TBS–Bray, Beck & Koetter, CPA, P.A.
2005	Titusville, FL	TBS–Bray, Beck & Koetter, CPA, P.A.
2007	Orlando, FL	Tedder, James, Worden & Associates, P.A.

GREAT LAKES

1945	Janesville, WI	Established
1959	Elkhart, IN	Duncan Pedigo
		Holdeman, Chiddister & Co. (1970–1983)
1964	South Bend, IN	Price Flatley
		Bernth, Casper & Dennen (1978)
		Dincolo, Stump & Co. (1979)
1970	Rockford, IL	Skee, Pedersen & Stocking
		Pollard & Weeler (1978)
		Crone, Kipp, Blomgren & Co. (1977–1988)
		KPMG (1994)
		Coopers and Lybrand
		BDO Seidman (2006)
1970	Barrington/Schaumburg, IL	Putta & Kelsey
1970	Crystal Lake, IL	Putta & Kelsey
1972–1997	Joliet, IL	Grumley, Dickey, Thornton & Clark
1978–1983	LaPorte, IN	Bernth, Casper & Dennen (1978)
1982–1985	Indianapolis, IN	Fowler + Suttles & Co. (1950–1982)
1983	Goshen, IN	Holdeman, Chiddister & Co. (1970–1983)
		Stauffer & Co. (2006)
1985	Chicago, IL	Ike Oberman
		HRB–Berg, DeMarco, Lewis, Sawatski & Co. (2000)
		HRB–Friedman, Eisenstein, Raemer & Schwartz (2000)
		Cottle & Cottle
		TBS–Altschuler, Melvoin & Glasser, LLP (2005)
		Checkers, Simon & Rosner
1990	Madison, WI	Fitzpatrick & Roberts
		Houghton Taplick (1993)
1991–1997	Olympia Fields, IL	Wilkes, Besterfield & Co (1925–1991)
2001	Milwaukee, WI	James & Scott
1997	Mokena, IL	Established (Merged Olympia Fields and Joliet)
2005	Deerfield, WI	TBS–Altschuler, Melvoin & Glasser, LLP (2005)
		Berger, Goldstein & Veatch
		Rich & Nadler

Appendixes

Year	Office	Merger or Other
MID ATLANTIC		
1984	Richmond, VA	A.M. Pullen & Company (1908–1984)
		Cheely Burcham Eddens Rokenbrod & Carroll, PC (2002)
2000	Baltimore, MD	HRB–C.W. Amos & Company (1921–2000)
2000	Bethesda, MD	Keller Bruner & Company LLP
2000	Frederick, MD	Keller Bruner & Company LLP
2000	Alexandria, VA	Keller Bruner & Company LLP
2005	Timonium, MD	TBS–Walpert & Wolpoff, LLP (2005)
2005	Rockville, MD	TBS–Walpert & Wolpoff, LLP (2005)
NEW YORK		
1984	New York, NY	A.M. Pullen & Company (1947–1984)
		Mann, Brown & Company (1950–1984)
		Cahill, Larkin & Company (1980–1989)
		Edward Isaacs (1930–2000)
		TBS–Goldstein, Golub Kessler LLP (1964–2007)
1984 - 2002	Long Island, NY	A.M. Pullen & Company (1959–1984)
		Kolesar & Company (1988)
OHIO TBS		
2005	Akron, OH	TBS–Hausser + Taylor, LLP
2005	Canton, OH	TBS–Hausser + Taylor, LLP
2005	Cleveland, OH	TBS–Hausser + Taylor, LLP
2005	Columbus, OH	TBS–Hausser + Taylor, LLP
2005	Elyria, OH	TBS–Hausser + Taylor, LLP
PHILADELPHIA		
2000	Blue Bell, PA	HRB–Rudolph Palitz (1949-2000)
		Mantas, Ohliger, McGary & Quinn (2006)
2001	Cherry Hill, MJ	Technology Group (2001)
2005	Harrisburg, PA	Established

Year	Office	Merger or Other

SEATTLE

2001	Seattle, WA	Knight Vale & Gregory PLLC (1921–2001)
2001	Tacoma, WA	Knight Vale & Gregory PLLC (1921–2001)
2001	Olympia, WA	Knight Vale & Gregory PLLC (1921–2001)

SOUTHERN CALIFORNIA

1977	Arcadia/Pasadena, CA	Harmon & Company
1977	Orange/Anaheim/Irvine, CA	Harmon & Company
		Gillespie, LeFerve, Lokietz and Vuona (1993)
1978	San Diego, CA	West, Blue, Johnston and Turnquist
		See, Hodge, Gordon & Diamond (1983)
		HRG, Inc. (2000)
		TBS–Altschuler, Melvoin & Glasser, LLP, California
1981	Colton/San Bernadino/ Riverside, CA	Easley & Giroir

SOUTHERN NEW ENGLAND

1989	New Haven, CT	Cahill, Larkin & Company (1980–1989)
2000–2002	White Plains, NY	Edward Isaacs (1930–2000)
2001	Stamford, CT	Messina, Ceci, Archer & Company, P.C. (1985–2001)

UPPER MIDWEST

1978	Minneapolis, MN	Broeker Hendrickson & Co. (1946–1978)
1978	St. Paul, MN	Broeker Hendrickson & Co. (1946–1978)
		Anderson & Seiberlich (1980)
1978–1987	Fargo, ND	Broeker Hendrickson & Co. (1950–1978)
		Holtgrewe & Nelson (1980)
1978	Sioux Falls, SD	Broeker Hendrickson & Co. (1960–1978)
1978–2005	Pierre, SD	Broeker Hendrickson & Co. (1966–1978)
1978–1984	Watertown, SD	Broeker Hendrickson & Co. (1973–1978)
1978–1981	Worthingon, MN	Broeker Hendrickson & Co. (1978)
1980–1995	Stillwater, MN	Anderson & Seiberlich (1980)

Year	Office	Merger or Other
UPPER MIDWEST *(continued)*		
1978	Duluth, MN/Superior, WI	Broeker Hendrickson & Co. (1978)
		Stillman, Swanson & Co. Ltd (1968–1983)
		Sellwood, Bonderson & Co. (1990)
1978	Rochester, MN	Broeker Hendrickson & Co. (1958–1978)
1978–1983	Hibbing, MN	Broeker Hendrickson & Co.
1982	LaCrosse, WI	Frank Uhler Associates (1981–1982)
1982	Winona, MN	Frank Uhler Associates (1981–1982)
1982–2005	Rapid City, SD	Dunmire, Short & Co. (1941–1982)
1982–1991	Gillette, WY	Dunmire, Short & Co. (1941–1982)
		Legerski, Dooley & Company (1986)
1978–1985	Billings, MT	Broeker Hendrickson & Co. (1972–1978)
		Greteman, Adams & Co. (1976–1979)
1983–1996	Bloomington, MN–Operating	Established
		Mork & Co. (1986)
		Borowicz & Associates, P.A. (1990)
NATIONAL CREDIT UNIONS		
2001	Brisbane, CA	O'Rourke, Sacher & Moulton
2001	Los Angeles, CA	O'Rourke, Sacher & Moulton
2001	Belleveue, WA	O'Rourke, Sacher & Moulton
2001	Dallas, TX	O'Rourke, Sacher & Moulton
2001	Beverly, MA	O'Rourke, Sacher & Moulton
NORTHERN CALIFORNIA		
2005	Mountain View, CA	TBS–Altschuler, Melvoin & Glasser, LLP, California
PROVIDENT		
2005	Santa Monica, CA	TBS
2005	San Francisco, CA	TBS
RSM MCGLADREY NETWORK		
1988	Peoria, IL	Established

Year	Office	Merger or Other

SPECIALTY CONSULTING SERVICES

1988	Minneapolis, MN	Hubler/Swartz Consulting
2005	Various	TBS–CFO Advisory Services
2005	Various	TBS–Insurance Regulatory

RETIREMENT RESOURCES

1983–1985	Cedar Rapids, IA	Established MPACT
1985	Rockford, IL	The Pension Service Company (197–1985)
1998	Chicago, IL	HRB–Friedman Eisenstein Ramer and Schwartz (1998)
		TBS–Altschuler, Melvoin & Glasser, LLP (2005)
2000	Annapolis, MD	Turner Pension (1994-2000)
2005	Phoenix, AZ	TBS–Altschuler, Melvoin & Glasser, LLP (2005)

CAPITAL MARKETS

2001	Costa Mesa, CA	EquiCO

EMPLOYER SERVICES

2001–2007	Atlanta, GA	MyBenefitSource
		Huber, Oros & Company LLC (2004)
		PWR Insurance Services, Inc. (2004)

FINANCIAL PROCESS OUTSOURCING

1994	Skokie, IL	Established
		Franchise Service Options of Madison, LLC (2005)
		Restaurant Reporting +Plus LTD (2005)
		Astute BPO Solutions Private Limited (2005)

CENTRAL OFFICE

1926–1960	Cedar Rapids, IA	
1960–1996	Rock Island/Davenport, IA	
1996	Minneapolis/Bloomington, MN	

Appendix Two

Historical Timeline

Our history is interesting and varied – a legacy of pride for all those associated with RSM McGladrey and McGladrey & Pullen. Here are some of our highlights, along with other points of interest.

1926	• Ira B. McGladrey starts his own accounting firm, I. B. McGladrey Co., in Cedar Rapids, Iowa. • Alan Greenspan, Economist and Chairman of the Federal Reserve Board, was born.
1929	• Stock market crashes. • Great Depression begins. • **McGladrey lays off no one; instead he hires additional accountants.**
1934	• McGladrey employee George Hansen begins offering clients management advice, later called consulting services. • Securities Exchange Act is passed, establishing the Securities and Exchange Commission.
1942	• World War II stalls growth of the firm; many clients and employees (including McGladrey himself) called to military service.
1949	• Ira McGladrey helps lead American Institute of Certified Public Accountants to adopt Statement 23, requiring public auditors to express or disclaim an opinion on financial statements written in the report. • Wall Street's Dow Jones Industrial Average closes December 31 at 200.13, with its first close above 200 in 10 years.

1952	• Ira McGladrey dies at age 68.
• The Bureau of Internal Revenue becomes the IRS.
1957	• **McGladrey, Hansen and Dunn opens its tenth office.**
• President Eisenhower sends federal troops into Little Rock, Arkansas, to protect 9 black students who enrolled in Little Rock Central High School.
1963	• Employee number #100, Lionel Lenz, is hired.
• President John F. Kennedy is assassinated in Dallas, Texas.
1964	• **Firm is founding partner of DRM International, an affiliation of international accounting and consulting firms.**
1973	• **McGladrey, Hansen and Dunn is a leader of Associated Accounting Firms International, which includes many other similar firms (Broeker Hendrickson, A.M. Pullen, and Moss Adams).**
• Financial Accounting Standards Board is formed.
1977	• **Diane McNulty becomes first woman named to firm's partnership.**
• Elvis Presley dies at age 42.
1978	• Firm merges with Broeker Hendrickson and Co. to become McGladrey Hendrickson and Co., one of the Midwest's largest regional firms.
• The government Employee Retirement Income Security Act of 1974 is extended to include 401(k) accounts, named after a section of the IRS code.
1984	• **Firm merges with A.M. Pullen and Co., expanding presence to the Southeast, and is now called McGladrey, Hendrickson & Pullen.**
• **Firm passes $100 million in revenue**
• The breakup of AT&T takes place as the telecommunications giant is broken up and 8 new companies were formed, including US West and Sprint.

Appendixes

1987	• Firm is renamed McGladrey & Pullen. • Black Monday on Wall Street occurs – stocks plummet on markets around the world.
1988	• **McGladrey & Pullen organizes the McGladrey Network, which grows to include nearly 100 independent accounting and consulting firms in the U.S. and Puerto Rico.** • **Employee #10,000 is hired.** • Chicago gives the Cubs the right to install lights on Wrigley Field.
1989	• **McGladrey & Pullen expands to New York and Connecticut.** • Ernst & Whinney and Arthur Young & Company announce merge, the first merger of the Big 8 firms. • Deloite, Haskins & Sells and Touche Ross merge for the second Big 8 merger.
1996	• **McGladrey & Pullen establishes headquarters in Bloomington, Minnesota.** • All the nearly 16,000 public companies nationwide are required to file their financial reports electronically with the SEC, using EDGAR, the Electronic Data Gathering, Analysis, and Retrieval system.
1997	• **Firm board of directors elects the Office of the Managing Partner to lead the firm.** • Coopers & Lybrand and Price Waterhouse merge to form the Big 5.
1999	• **McGladrey & Pullen sells its non-attest services to H&R Block, creating RSM McGladrey Inc., a wholly owned subsidiary of Block. RSM McGladrey and McGladrey & Pullen remain affiliated as an alternative practice structure.** • **Employee #20,000, Sushurt Pophali, is hired.** • The Dow Jones Industrial Average closes above 11,000, just 24 trading days after passing 10,000.
2000	• **McGladrey expands to Kansas City, Dallas, Denver, Philadelphia, Boston, Baltimore, Washington D.C., and Buffalo, and grows in Chicago, Phoenix and New York City.** • United States Supreme Court renders its decision which results in the election of George W. Bush, President of the United States

2001	• McGladrey, with about 2,400 employees in 100 offices, celebrates 75 years as a top firm serving midsized companies. • The SEC inquiry into Enron Corp. becomes a formal investigation.
2002	• **McGladrey expands into a business services firm with capital markets, payroll, retirement resources, and financial planning process outsourcing.** • The Sarbanes Oxley Act is enacted. • Arthur Andersen discontinues operations as a result of the Enron scandal. Big 5 becomes Big 4.
2005	• With the acquisition of the Tax & Business Services division of American Express, McGladrey becomes the first firm, other than the Big 4, to pass $1.0 billion in revenue. • Hurricane Katrina hits the Gulf Coast in one of the biggest tragedies in U.S. history.
2006	• **Teresa Gable becomes 100th female partner.**
2007	• McGladrey continues to grow, employing more than 8,000 employees. • Annual revenue surpasses $1.4 billion. • Employee #40,000, Michael Ko, is hired.

Appendix Three

Senior Management and Managing Partners

Name	Year
Managing Partner - M & P	
Ira B McGladrey	1926–1952
George Hansen	1952–1966
Ivan Bull	1966–1982
Jack Wahlig	1982–1989
LeRoy Martin	1989–1997
Mark Scally (1)	1997–1999
Tom Rotherham (1)	1997–1999
Bob Jensen (1)	1997–1998
Bill Travis	1999–2006
Mitch Gorochow (Interim)	2007
Dave Scudder	2007–
CEO - RSM McGladrey, Inc.	
Mark Scally	1999–2000
Tom Rotherham	2000–2003
Steve Tait	2003–
Operations (2)	
George Hansen	1939–1952
Keith Dunn	1939–1960
Ivan Bull	1959–1966
Dave Wentworth	1966–1981
Warren Bolmgren	1978–1981

Name	Year
Operations (2) *(continued)*	
Hal Quill	1981–1990
Jack Heins	1981–1985
Frank Booth	1984–1986
LeRoy Martin	1985–1989
Tom Rotherham	1985–1989
John Bryant	1989–1992
Jim Fussell	1989–1997
Mark Scally	1985–1997
Van Thompson	1985–1990
John Holdeman	1985–1986
Dick Letsche	1989–1997
Larry Bildstein	1992–1997
Bob Jensen	1985–1997
Jim Blayney	1990–1995
Bob Jensen	1998–2002
Mike Kirley	1999–2008
Craig Damos	1999–2000
Duane Tyler	2000–2002
Jim Blayney	2002–2005
Sabry Heakal	2005–2006
Doug Opheim	2006–

Name	Year	Name	Year
TAX LEADER		**CHIEF FINANCIAL OFFICER** (3)	
Roy Barnes	1960–1969	Jay Vondehaar	1985–1986
Paul Cremer	1969–1978	Jim Fussell	1986–1989
Tom Cronin	1978–1984	Tom Rotherham	1989–1990
John Bryant	1984–1989	Hal Quill	1990–1991
Roger Neumann	1989	John Bryant	1991–1997
Joe Gevock	1989–1995	Tom Rotherham	1997–1999
Bill Heittritter	1995–2001	Doug Opheim	1999–2003
Kimpa Moss	2001–2005	Rene Ordogne	2003–
Mike Metz	2005–		
		CHIEF INFORMATION OFFICER (3)	
CONSULTING LEADER		Galen Vetter	1995–1998
Bill Osmundson	1965–197	Doug Opheim	1998–2004
Larry Dowell	1972–1981	Joe Topinka	2004–2008
Bob Jensen	1981–1985	Bob Gerardi	2008–
Larry Dowell	1985–2000		
Audie Dunham	2000–2003	**CHIEF HR OFFICER** (3)	
Randy Siemsen	2003–2006	Cheryl Fells	1994–1997
Tom Dobosenski	2006–	Susan Goldstein (Lewis)	1997–1998
		Kathy Kenny	1998–2005
AUDIT LEADER		Sue Mulkern/ Linda Brennan	2005–2007
Leo Burger	1961–1973	Kimpa Moss	2007–
John Hoyt	1973–1978		
LeRoy Martin	1978–1983	**CHIEF MARKETING OFFICER** (3)	
Tom Rotherham	1983–1985	Larry Bildstein	1998–2001
Sabry Heakel	1985–1995	Louise Sharer	2001–2005
Tom Rotherham	1995–1997	Art Smith	2005–2007
Bill Travis	1997–2003	Mark Audino	2007–
LeRoy Dennis	2003–2007		
Dave Scudder	2007–		

(1) Beginning in 1997 to 1999, there was an Office of Managing Partner.
(2) Individuals listed are those leaders who were responsible for economic units and reported directly to the Managing Partner or CEO. Titles were Executive Partner, Regional Managing Partner, Senior Vice President and Chief Operating Officers.
(3) The internal functional leaders are shown from the time the position reported to the managing partner or CEO.

Appendix Four

Board Members

Name	Year	Name	Year	Name	Year
Board Members—Chairmen		**Board Members** (continued)		**Board Members** (continued)	
Ivan Bull	1956–1981	Byron Ross	1976–1980	Curt Anderson	1983–1984
Dave Wentworth	1967–1981	Jay Vonderhaar	1976–1980	Dick McMahon	1983–1985
Jack Wahlig	1981–1990	Bill Brauer	1976–1980	LeRoy Martin	1984–1987
LeRoy Martin	1989–1997	Jerry Hall	1977–1981	Mike McGee	1984–1988
Mark Scally	1997–2000	Bill Osmundson	1978–1982	Rollie Emerson	1984–1985
Bill Travis	1999–2007	Jim West	1978–1982	Clark Burritt	1984–1986
Tom Rotherham	2000–2003	Warren Bolmgren	1978–1981	Tom Horne	1984–1987
Dave Scudder	2007–	LeRoy Martin	1978–1983	Jim Muller	1984–1988
		Mert Hanson	1979–1983	John Sanderson	1984–1988
Board Members		Jim Kennedy	1980–1984	Jim Murray	1984–1989
George Hansen	1956 (1)	Don Rieck	1980–1984	Tom Cronin	1985–1989
Keith Dunn	1956 (1)	Dick Letsche	1980–1985	Dave Schmidt	1985–1985
Leo Burger	1956 (1)	Hal Quill	1980–1981	Jerry Chicoine	1985–1986
Frank Cover	1956 (1)	John Bryant	1981–1985	Vern Nelson	1985–1989
		Mark Scally	1981–1984	Lowell Garner	1986–1990
		Duane Butt	1982–1986	Joe Gevock	1986–1989
		Clark Hollingsworth	1982–1986	Jim Blayney	1986–1990

Name	Year	Name	Year	Name	Year
Board Members (continued)		**Board Members** (continued)		**Board Members** (continued)	
Bob Early	1987–1991	Steve Hammes	1996–2000	Don Lipari	2007–2009
Dick Letsche	1987–1989	Doug Opheim	1996–1999	Mendel Nudelman	2007–2010
Paul Floyd	1988–1992	Jeff Cannon	1997–2000	Jim Knudsen	2007–2011
Bob McNairy	1988–1992	Bob Lindeman	1997–2001	Mike Dubin	2007–2011
Bob Sipple	1988–1992	Pat Murphy	1997–2001	Tim Tiefenthaler	2007–2011
Duane Butt	1989–1991	Jim Blayney	1998–2002		
Bill Heittritter	1989–1993	Gary Kramer	1998–2002		
Bill Schneider	1989–1993	Gordon Opland	1998–2002		
Don Decker	1989–1992	Bob Early	1999–2000		
Gary Smith	1989–1993	Jay Zack	1999–2003		
Tim Frick	1990–1994	Don Natenstedt	2000–2004		
Gerry Hanggi	1990–1994	John Sanders	2000–2004		
Clark Hollingsworth	1990–1994	Dan Brooks	2000–2004		
Dave Parkinson	1991–1995	Steve Bauer	2001–2005		
Bill Travis	1991–1995	Glenn Bougie	2002–2005		
Craig Damos	1992–1996	Kaye Lauritsen	2002–2006		
Jim Fitzpatrick	1992–1996	Mitch Gorochow	2002–2007		
Peter Siciliano	1992–1996	Joe Adams	2002–2004		
Kay Hagarty	1993–1997	Jeff Johannesen	2003–2007		
Roger Hendren	1993–1997	Bill Roche	2002–2006		
Jim Murray	1993–1997	Kristi Kennedy	2004–2008		
Bill Alexander	1994–1998	Joe Mazza	2004–2008		
Ron Barzen	1994–1998	Tony Ceci	2005–2009		
Duane Tyler	1994–1998	Dave Scudder	2005–2007		
Mike Martin	1995–1999	Tom Losey	2006–2010		
DeWayne Scheer	1995–1999	Deb Lockwood	2006–2010		
Karen Bowman	1996–2000	Bill Travis	2006–2010		

(1) *In 1956, the Partnership Agreement was revised to provide orderly transfer of both ownership and control. George Hansen and Keith Dunn became minority owners and created the Management Committee (now called the Board of Directors).*

Appendix Five

Quotes from RSM CEOs and McGladrey & Pullen Managing Partners

Ira B. McGladrey: 1926–1952

"This company was founded on three enduring values: provide outstanding client service, treat employees well, and do your work honestly and ethically."

Ira B. McGladrey

George Hansen: 1952–1966

"Dedicate yourselves to serving your real clients—individuals. Even though they pay our fees, corporations and other profit and nonprofit entities are pseudo-clients. They are instruments created by people to serve people. If we concentrate on serving the needs of people, our service opportunities become almost limitless."

George Hanson

Ivan Bull: 1966–1981

"We provide benefits to our clients by helping them obtain better results, by providing credibility for financial reports, by helping create order out of disorder, by helping assure compliance and by providing comfort. We want an internal climate that demands integrity, causes acceptance of high performance goals and encourages supportive relationships among all people in the firm."

Ivan Bull

Jack Wahlig: 1981–1989

"This firm [McGladrey] was built by a bunch of characters—not corporate types. There were a lot of mavericks back then. They were just good client servers who busted their backs for clients."

Jack Wahlig

LeRoy Martin: 1989–1997

"Having good people is the most essential criterion for a successful office. I have always believed that if you have good people, everything else follows."

LeRoy Martin

Mark Scally: 1997–2000

"We are in business, A) To help our clients succeed, and the reason that is important is that many of our clients cannot be as successful as they want to be without the help of our firm – read that as the help of you. B) To provide a workplace for all of us to develop our talents and live a meaningful energized life with McGladrey and Pullen."

Mark Scally

Tom Rotherham: 2000–2003

"Our ingenuity, creativity, and ability to approach the future with eager and open minds inspires our people to do likewise."

Tom Rotherham

Bill Travis: 2000–2006

Upon McGladrey's seventy-fifth anniversary: "Like so many of our clients, we were once a small, entrepreneurial firm with dreams of greatness. We have come a long way in seventy-five years. Today, we are in the midst of significant growth which will result in our achieving a truly national presence in our industry."

Bill Travis

Steve Tait: 2003–Present

"Our corporate values are respect, integrity, teamwork, client focus, and excellence. These values helped form the culture that Ira McGladrey established for the firm he founded in 1926, and they still accurately reflect how we work and serve our clients today."

Steve Tait

Dave Scudder: 2007–Present

"Today our firm employs over 600 partners and 8,000 employees from coast to coast. Our name has changed through the years as we've added many new people and new locations, and made several significant acquisitions and mergers. But the constant through all of those changes has been the values of the people we bring in and the devotion to serving the needs of the middle market with the same integrity and dedication that our founding partners had."

Dave Scudder

Appendixes

Our Core Values

CLIENT-FOCUSED
~ We are passionate about helping our clients. Their success is a key measure of our success.

RESPECT
~ We treat each other with respect and dignity, recognizing that innovation springs from unique perspectives.

EXCELLENCE
~ We take pride in doing our best in everything we undertake. We embrace change to learn and grow.

TEAMWORK
~ Collaboration and full participation by everyone make us stronger and allow us to serve clients better.

INTEGRITY
~ We are honest and ethical in everything we do.